VANISHING SPECIES

The wildlife art of Laura Regan

Cedco Publishing Company
2955 Kerner Blvd.
San Rafael, CA 94901

Publisher: Charles E. Ditlefsen
Concept: Mary L. Sullivan
Editorial direction: Robert Young
Design & art direction: Donald Scott Macdonald
Assistant art director: Joel Ibsen
Production artist: Kelly Gennert
Typesetting: ProType Graphics, Inc.

Composed in **LITHOS**, Tekton, *Bodoni*

Vanishing Species; the Wildlife Art of Laura Regan published by
Cedco Publishing Company
2955 Kerner Blvd., San Rafael, CA 94901 U.S.A.

Printed in Korea

ISBN 1-55912-377-X

First Edition

ABOUT THE WRITER

Michelle D. Minnich is a freelance writer working in Troy, Ohio, who writes for local and national clients in both the publishing and business fields.

She holds a bachelor's degree in public relations from Ohio State University's School of Journalism, where she graduated in 1986.

In her free time Ms. Minnich is a volunteer involved with local wildlife rehabilitation centers where she helps injured, sick and orphaned animals. In addition, she also works with helping the homeless in Columbus, Ohio, where she has received an award for her contributions.

ABOUT THE RESEARCH ZOOLOGIST

Laurie Ann Macdonald (B.A., University of Oregon; M.S., University of South Florida) is a freelance wildlife zoologist living in St. Petersburg, Florida, whose work involves both research and private consulting. She specializes in the study and protection of the gopher tortoise (Gopherus polyphemus), a species in decline due to the rapid loss of habitat in the southeastern United States.

Much of Ms. Macdonald's time is dedicated to volunteer environmental advocacy on the regional, national, and international levels. Among other volunteer positions, she currently serves as the Sierra Club Chair for Endangered Species and Biological Diversity. She is also on the management team for the Sierra Club's Center for Environmental Innovation. When she is not working, Ms. Macdonald enjoys nature around the world by bicycling, kayaking and hiking.

SPECIAL ACKNOWLEDGEMENTS

The publisher would like to thank the following groups for their assistance in the preparation of the manuscript for this book: The Allyn Museum, the American Museum of Natural History, the Busch Gardens Conservation Department and the International Crane Foundation.

In addition, we wish to thank Eric Anderson, Marty Crump, Arthur Echternacht, Peter Feinsinger, George Heinrich, Margo McKnight, Paul Moler, Chris Schleh and Stacey Small for their individual contributions in verifying the accuracy of the information presented in Vanishing Species.

CRES, the Center for the Reproduction of Endangered Species, was established in 1975 as the worldwide conservation and research arm of the renowned San Diego Zoo. As a lead organization involved with international wildlife conservation, its mission is to help preserve animal species threatened with extinction.

Working with wildlife centers and zoos all over the world, CRES is applying medical techniques to help in the reproduction of rare animal species such as cheetahs, condors and gorillas.

There are between five million to thirty million species on our planet. But, as fields and forests surrender to the growing demands of humanity, many of earth's species are clinging to life. By tearing apart the earth's ecosystems we are blindly unraveling the complex web of life by which we all survive. It is estimated that three-quarters of the world's animal species could vanish in the next twenty-five years. For example, less than thirty northern white rhinos remain in the wild with another twelve in captivity and only seventy California condors exist in all the world.

CRES is dedicated to preserving the world's precious wildlife for future generations. If you want to receive information on how you can help CRES, please write:

CRES Development Office
Zoological Society of San Diego
P.O. Box 551
San Diego, CA 92112-0551

CONTENTS

ABOUT THE ARTIST

Laura Regan was born in Vancouver, British Columbia in 1950. When she was three her family moved from Canada to the San Francisco Bay Area where she grew up. After attending Notre Dame High School and the College of San Mateo, she studied graphic design at the Maryland Institute College of Art in Baltimore. Laura established a career in the advertising field until 1975 when she began exhibiting and selling her paintings full time.

Laura Regan has become widely known for her clean, rich, contemporary style which she creates by painting in either oil or gouache. She has had many one-woman exhibits in the United States including shows at The Lawrence Hall of Science at the University of California in Berkeley, at the Two Plus Two Gallery in New Orleans, and at Neiman Marcus in San Francisco. In addition, her works are widely held in private and public collections. Her artwork is extensively reproduced for commercial use and appears on items such as calendars, greeting cards and collector's plates.

Besides the work you see in *Vanishing Species* Laura Regan has also illustrated *Welcome to the Green House* written by Jane Yolen (Putnam) and is currently working on *Sunsong* written by Jean Marzollo (Harper Collins).

Laura Regan lives with her husband and children in Woodside, California.

INTRODUCTION

The saying goes that variety is the spice of life. Today we know that variety is the substance of life on this planet. **Vanishing species; the Wildlife Art of Laura Regan** offers the opportunity to more deeply appreciate and understand the vibrancy in this variety of life.

Harvard professor E.O. Wilson said that scientists can make better estimates of the number of stars in the universe than they can of the number of species on earth. Today, many of these species are being eliminated before they can be counted. What place do these vanishing animals and plants play in the tapestry of life? What could they offer us in our knowledge of the world or in understanding ourselves?

Time and time again in the text of this book the words "habitat loss" are used to describe the primary threat to a species. Habitat loss results from many different processes. Directly, habitat is lost through urban growth, agricultural expansion and logging. Indirectly, it vanishes through less dramatic means such as fragmentation of large tracts of wild land into areas too small to support the biological diversity necessary for the survival of certain species. Specific threats to certain animals, overhunting, predator control and the illegal trade in furs, ivory and live animals exacerbate the problems caused by habitat loss.

Many organizations, government agencies and individuals are at work to save threatened habitats and to protect the world's biological diversity. *Vanishing Species* cites many of these efforts and gives specific information as to the current status of the protection and preservation of species included in this book. In the race to study and save these unique animals, it is difficult to know, or in some cases agree upon, what the current facts are. The what, when, where and how of these animals' existence can only be established through extensive research. The research in *Vanishing Species* has been done by zoologist/ecologist Laurie Ann Macdonald and in turn was reviewed by selected experts in each field through the auspices of CRES, (the Center for the Reproduction of Endangered Species), an internationally respected arm of the renowned San Diego Zoo.

Flowing through this book, tying animal to environment, bringing to life the diverse inhabitants of our world, are the works of artist Laura Regan. Her oil and gouache paintings have been displayed throughout the United States. Many of them have been purchased by enthusiastic collectors. Others have appeared on posters, in calendars and in books illustrated by her. From elephant to butterfly, each animal is equally worthy of the artist's attention as each should be in our efforts to preserve and protect them. One hundred and forty years ago, Native American Chief Seattle spoke of this when he said, "Humankind does not weave the web of life; we are merely a strand in it. Whatever we do to the web, we do to ourselves."

Vanishing Species

SCARLET MACAW
Ara macao

THE TRADE IN WILD BIRDS IS BIG BUSINESS IN MANY COUNTRIES. THIS TRADE BY ITSELF CAN ENDANGER A SPECIES IF THE VOLUME IS EXCESSIVE.

The scarlet macaw is probably the best known of all South American parrots. Unfortunately, catching a glimpse of this brightly-colored bird in the wild is rare. Hunting and collecting have removed macaws from areas of human settlement. In addition, the tropical environment where they live is rapidly being destroyed.

The brilliant colors of scarlet macaws actually serve as a camouflage for the birds. Macaws live in dense forests choosing high treetops for cover where there is little light. Without light, their green feathers blend with the forest foliage and their colors appear dull, making them hard to spot for even the most experienced parrot watcher. The best time to observe these glorious birds is when they are flying from tree to tree in search of food.

Macaws have strong beaks which allow them to crack the hard shells of a variety of nuts. They also like to eat seeds, fruits and berries.

Scarlet macaws are generally seen in pairs, family groups or small flocks of up to thirty birds. Bonding between a pair of macaws is so strong that even when flying, their wings almost touch. They nest deep inside hollow trees where one or two eggs are laid and incubated for 30 days. Macaw chicks are born blind and helpless and require a great deal of initial care from their parents.

Efforts to stop deforestation are important to the survival of the scarlet macaw. However, the issue of trade in wild birds is also critical for these parrots. Some countries do not prohibit export of parrots because of the money this trade brings into their economy. During the 1970s the worldwide trade of parrots was exceptionally high. Since then, new laws and strict quarantine measures have been adopted by many countries to help save these and other wild birds.

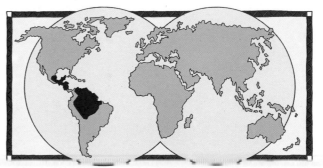

Range: Tropical regions of South America.

CHEETAH
Acinonyx jubatus

PEOPLE IN ANCIENT EGYPT, SUMERIA, ASSYRIA, EUROPE AND INDIA TAMED CHEETAHS AND USED THEM TO RUN DOWN GAME. THE CHEETAH WAS USUALLY HOODED WHEN TAKEN OUT FOR THE CHASE, THEN FREED WHEN THE GAME WAS IN SIGHT.

Slender and sleek, the cheetah has been clocked at speeds of up to 70 miles (112 km) per hour. While such bursts cannot be maintained for more than a few hundred yards, this still makes the cheetah the fastest land mammal. Unfortunately, the cheetah is not able to outrun the threats that may cause its extinction. Human influences are a major factor in the decline of cheetah populations. In addition, one theory suggests that a lack of genetic variation may also pose a threat to the species.

Studies have demonstrated that compared to other species the cheetah has an unusually low degree of genetic variation which could result in problems related to inbreeding. Currently it is limited food supply and high predation of their offspring that make cheetah populations vulnerable in the wild.

The cheetah's body is 3.5 to 5 feet (105-150 cm) long, with a tail adding another 2.5 feet (75 cm) in length. Weight ranges between 77 to 160 pounds (35-72 kg).

Cheetahs live alone or in small groups either consisting of a female with her cubs or in small all-male groups (usually brothers). A mother cheetah carries her cubs for 90 to 95 days. The average number of cubs that are born ranges from three to five, but occasionally there can be as many as eight. The babies are weaned at three to six months when the mother teaches them to hunt for gazelles, impalas, zebras, and other hoofed mammals.

Cheetahs are listed as an endangered species by the United States Department of the Interior (USDI), vulnerable by the International Union for Conservation of Nature (IUCN), and are subject to restrictions under the Convention on International Trade in Endangered Species (CITES). While these organizations are protecting cheetah populations, research and direct action are needed to strengthen the cheetahs' reproductive ability, increase their resistance to disease and make them more resilient to changes in their natural environment.

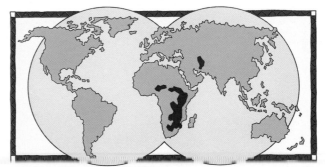

Range: Africa to India, except for the tropical forest zone and central Sahara.

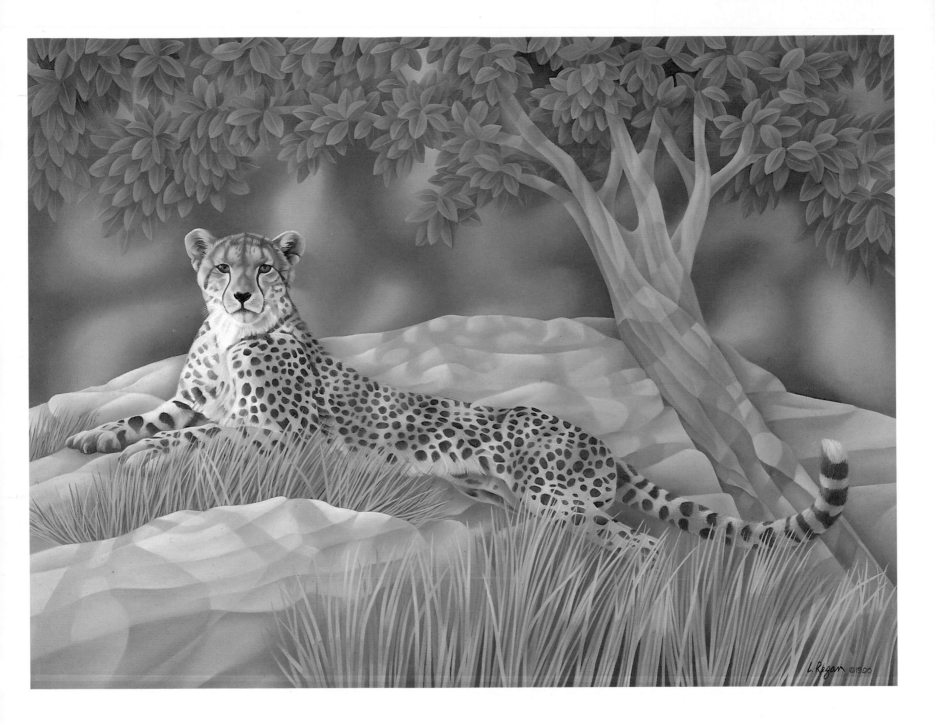

L. Regan ©1990

MOST AUTHORITIES AGREE THAT THE GIANT PANDA IS MORE CLOSELY RELATED TO THE BEAR RATHER THAN THE RACCOON FAMILY.

Giant pandas are among the most popular animals in zoos and are one of the most cherished animals on earth. But because there are so few in existence, displaying them has become highly controversial. Proponents say panda exhibits protect the species because admission charges raise funds for conservation efforts. Others argue that pandas should be kept in China, their native habitat, and held in captivity only as part of a conservation program.

Giant pandas are easily recognized by their round faces, white eye patches and little black ears. They reach a height of five feet (153 cm) and weigh an average of 165-350 pounds (75-160 kg) when mature. Their facial features are a result of well developed chewing muscles and expanded skull features around the eyes. The forefoot has an unusual modification thought to aid in grasping bamboo stems.

Bamboo shoots are the primary food in the panda diet, although they also eat other plants such as gentians, irises, crocuses and tufted grasses. Occasionally, they hunt for fish and small rodents. They spend 10 to 12 hours a day feeding, usually in a sitting position with a forepaw free to manipulate their food.

Pandas live in forests with dense stands of bamboo, spending most of their time alone in marked territories. Mating generally occurs from March to May when females have a single fertile period of 12 to 25 days. However, peak receptivity lasts only one to five days and pandas usually have just one cub. This limited reproductive cycle contributes to the difficulty of successful breeding in captivity.

Today, only 1,000 giant pandas are thought to exist. The species is threatened by poachers, natural periodic die-off of their food source (bamboo) and human encroachment. The giant panda is classified as endangered by the United States Department of the Interior (ISDU), rare by the International Union for the Conservation of Nature (IUCN) and is protected by the Convention on International Trade in Endangered Species (CITES). Pandas receive complete legal protection from the Chinese government, and cooperative field investigations have been conducted by the Chinese government, the World Wildlife Fund, and the Center for Reproduction of Endangered Species (CRES) of the Zoological Society of San Diego in an attempt to learn more about this vulnerable rare species.

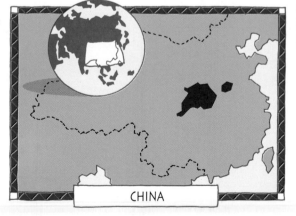

CHINA

The male panda is a fairly docile animal preferring to nibble on the tenderest leaves of bamboo branches. However, the female can be very aggressive & has jaws so strong that she can easily chew through a bamboo branch a couple of inches thick. The panda that I have painted here is definitely a male! — L.R.

LEOPARD "BLACK PANTHER"
Panthera pardus

LEOPARDS ARE USUALLY ACTIVE AT NIGHT. DURING THE DAY THEY REST IN THE BRANCHES OF TREES, IN DENSE VEGETATION OR AMONG ROCKS.

*A*lthough better able to adapt to the presence of people than the tiger, the leopard is still confronted with many of the same threats caused by coexistence with man. Humans threaten leopard populations by invading their habitat, trophy hunting and killing them for preying on livestock. Leopards suffered the same decline as other wild cats in the 1960s when they were killed in large quantities for their luxurious fur.

"Black panthers" are actually a melanistic form (color variant) of the leopard. In fact, if the lighting is right, a pattern of leopard spots can be seen despite the black pelage. They reach a body length of more than 6 feet (183 cm) with a tail that stretches more than 3.5 feet (107 cm). Males can weigh as much as 198 pounds (90 kg) and females may weigh up to 152 pounds (69 kg).

The strength of leopards is impressive. They are able to overcome much larger animals and carry their prey into a tree for eating. They are accomplished stalkers, approaching their quarry as close as possible then leaping to seize the animal by the throat.

Their diet is varied, but leopards prefer small to medium-sized ungulates (deer, impala, gazelles, wild goats and domestic livestock). They also will eat monkeys and baboons, and may switch to rodents and birds if necessary.

Leopards are solitary animals, although males have been seen helping females care for their young. Female leopards have litters of two to three cubs every year or two. Births occur in caves, crevices, hollow trees or thickets. Full size and sexual maturity is reached around the third year.

The United States lists the leopard as endangered throughout most of its range, and threatened in the remainder. The International Union for the Conservation of Nature (IUCN) also lists the panther as threatened. While the United States does not allow the importation of leopards for commercial purposes, it does allow [as accepted by the Convention on International Trade in Endangered Species (CITES)] the importation of trophy animals from areas where the animals are listed as threatened.

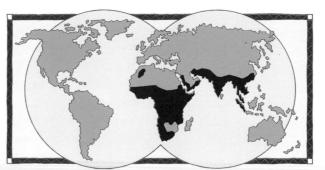

Range: Africa, Arabian Peninsula to southeastern Siberia. Commonly found in moist, dense forests.

African Elephant

Loxodonta africana

JUST AS HUMANS ARE RIGHT OR LEFT HANDED, ELEPHANTS ARE RIGHT OR LEFT TUSKED. THEREFORE THE DOMINANT TUSK WILL BE ROUNDED OFF AND WILL DIFFER IN LENGTH FROM THE LESS USED ONE.

Ivory tusks are the most magnificent feature of the massive African elephant, yet tragically, they are leading to the demise of this species. The threat to elephants can be attributed directly to humans. Whether the elephant is considered a valuable source of income or seen as a nuisance to farmers, people have been cruelly killing these animals for centuries, often taking only the tusks and leaving the rest. African elephants suffer additional losses as humans continue to fragment their habitat.

African elephants, the largest living land animal, can reach a height of 13 feet (400 cm) and can weigh as much as 8 tons (7,250 kg). The elephant's trunk is a modified nose, forehead and upper lip which contains 40,000 muscles. The trunk is extremely dexterous and is used for gathering food, lifting water to the mouth, fighting and to show affection by tenderly caressing other elephants.

It takes more than 300 pounds (136 kg) per day of grasses, leaves, herbs, bark and other browse to keep an elephant fed. About 18 out of every 24 hours is spent foraging for food. As elephants continue to be forced out of their native habitat and feed upon farmers' crops, this immense appetite puts them in danger.

While elephant herds vary in size they generally are comprised of females with young. Adult males join the females only during mating. The gestation period for an elephant is two years and it can be several more years before the baby is weaned.

As forests and grasslands where they roam are being destroyed for human use and the demand for ivory continues, the elephants' future is doubtful. Recently, however, conservation efforts have increased to include international programs to raise funds and carry out research by the International Union for Conservation of Nature (IUCN), the World Wildlife Fund, the Center for Reproduction of Endangered Species (CRES) of the Zoological Society of San Diego, the New York Zoological Society, and other private groups. The United States established an African Elephant Conservation Act, and in 1989 completely banned the importation of ivory. Elephants also are protected under the Convention on International Trade in Endangered Species (CITES) regulations.

Much remains to be done in terms of habitat management, working with local economies and eliminating worldwide demand for elephant ivory if the species is to survive.

Range: Africa south of the Sahara.

GIRAFFE
Giraffa camelopardalis

TO GET A DRINK OF WATER, THE GIRAFFE MUST SPREAD ITS FRONT TWO LEGS ESPECIALLY FAR APART SO IT CAN STRETCH ITS LONG NECK TO THE GROUND. IN THIS POSITION, THE ANIMAL IS VULNERABLE TO PREDATORS.

Human predation and habitat loss are the major threats confronting the giraffe today. While native Africans kill giraffes for their meat, sinews (used in making bowstrings and musical instruments), and tough hide (which is made into shields), it was overhunting by European settlers and poaching by indigenous populations which dramatically reduced giraffe numbers. The conversion of the giraffes' habitat into farms is equally, if not more, threatening to the continued existence of this tall and graceful creature.

"The sight of these huge animals running remains in my vision as one of the most flowing, elegant movements I have ever seen," says zoologist Laurie Macdonald. "At a distance, a group of giraffes running looks like slow motion waves, the head and neck reaching forward and the body following, moving up underneath."

Giraffes are shy, timid and alert. Their long necks and keen senses give them the greatest range of vision of any terrestrial creature. Their lengthy legs not only support their heavy bodies and long necks, but they propel the animal at speeds up to 35 miles (56 cm) per hour. Despite their large feet, giraffes are able to walk only on solid ground. They become bogged down in swampy terrain and large rivers are barriers to them.

Giraffes live in dry savannahs and open woodland, usually where there is an abundance of acacia, mimosa and wild apricot trees. They feed for an average of 18 hours per day, the large individuals consuming up to 75 pounds (34 kg) daily. They are able to go without water for long periods of time but will drink regularly if consuming dry food.

During the dry months, a female giraffe will usually produce one offspring and occasionally twins. The mother is pregnant for 457 days before she gives birth to a baby which can be as tall as 6.5 feet (200 cm). Young giraffes stay with their mothers for 18 months and reach maturity at about four years.

Historically, overhunting and climatic change resulted in a great reduction in the distribution and numbers of giraffes causing the species to disappear from north Africa. During the past century it has been eliminated from most of western and southern Africa. Sizeable populations remain in Tanzania and adjacent areas where the giraffe relies upon game reserves with their watchful game wardens for protection from poachers.

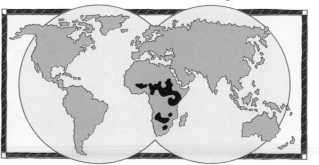

Range: Africa, south of the Sahara.

I was camping in the Ngorongoro Crater in Tanzania, East Africa when I saw these giraffes set against a tremendous blue-black thunderstorm sky. The lighting was quite eery. It seemed appropriate to capture these "other worldley" looking animals in this setting. — L.R.

GOLDEN TOAD
Bufo periglenes

THE FATE OF THE GOLDEN TOAD IS AN EXAMPLE OF HOW PRECARIOUS THE CIRCUMSTANCES ARE FOR RARE SPECIES. WITH SMALL POPULATIONS, THESE SPECIES DO NOT HAVE THE NUMBERS NECESSARY TO REBOUND FROM ADVERSE NATURAL OR HUMAN CAUSED DISTURBANCES.

Golden Toads are one of the rarest of all living species. They dwell in the "elfin" cloud forest near the continental divide of northern Costa Rica. Because they live underground (emerging only for a few months to breed), and because there are so few golden toads, little is known about them. No more than 1500 adult toads were observed during the 1987 breeding season and only eleven golden toads were seen by researchers between 1988 and 1990. It is believed natural factors occurring in their environment are threatening their numbers.

Male golden toads are brightly colored, a common characteristic of poisonous amphibians. This coloring is an indication of their skins' toxicity, a defense against predators. However, golden toads have been found with slit bellies and their insides eaten—a clue that at least one predator has learned how to feed on this poisonous prey.

The golden toad is endemic to the "elfin" cloud forests of Costa Rica. These elevated forests are bathed in mist from clouds and frequent rains, providing a moist habitat for the toads. The trees in the forests are gnarled and stunted with a dense covering of moss, ferns and air plants. Golden toads live in naturally formed cavities around tree roots and are thought to eat small invertebrates and insects living underground.

During the rainy season, April through June, water-filled hollows, puddles, ponds and other flooded areas serve as brood sites for the golden toad. They are congregate breeders, with many golden toads breeding in the same small pools of water. The tadpoles hatch about twenty-four hours after the eggs are spawned and require only a few weeks until they metamorphose into adult toads.

Golden toads are listed as endangered by the United States Department of the Interior (USDI) and the International Union for Conservation of Nature (IUCN). They are also protected by the Convention on International Trade in Endangered Species (CITES). Scientists who study this rare amphibian feel that it is too early to determine the cause of golden toads' declining numbers. They believe the species is either near extinction due to natural causes (such as drought affecting their breeding pools), or that adult toads are merely waiting for proper conditions to breed again. In either case, only time will show how many, if any, golden toads still exist in the wild.

Monteverde Cloud Forest Reserve

COSTA RICA

BRAZILIAN (MANED) THREE-TOED TREE SLOTH

Bradypus torquatus

THE THREE-TOED TREE SLOTH HAS EIGHT OR NINE NECK VERTEBRAE, UNLIKE MOST MAMMALS WHICH HAVE SEVEN. THESE EXTRA VERTEBRAE GIVE THE SLOTH GREATER FLEXIBILITY AND ENABLE IT TO TURN ITS HEAD 270 DEGREES.

The Atlantic coastal forest of Eastern Brazil, home to the three-toed tree sloth, is being rapidly cut down for lumber, charcoal production and to clear the land for plantations and cattle pastures, thereby threatening the sloth with extinction.

An unusual-looking animal, the sloth has a shaggy mane of coarse hair with a fine-textured fur underneath. As its name suggests, the three-toed sloth has three closely-spaced toes which end in long hooked claws. (There also is a species of two-toed sloths.) They are between 16 and 28 inches (41-71 cm) tall and have a short 3.5 inch (9 cm) tail. They weigh between five and twelve pounds (2.25-5.5 kg).

Sloths are solitary creatures who spend the majority of their lives in trees eating young leaves, tender twigs and buds. They especially favor the Cecropia tree.

Trees also provide a safe haven from predators. While sloths can move quickly through trees (and even swim well), they move at a turtle's pace on the ground. Therefore, sloths rarely descend from their tree, doing so only a couple times a week to relieve waste and move to a different tree. If they are threatened, they will slash out with their claws.

Females have one baby after a gestation period of five to six months. Although the young stop nursing at three to four weeks, they depend on the mother for another five months. Young sloths are carried on the mother's abdomen or cling to her back or arms.

Deforestation is jeopardizing the existence of all three species of three-toed sloths. The Brazilian three-toed tree sloth is classified as endangered by the United States and the International Union for Conservation of Nature (IUCN). It is protected by law in Brazil, but only a tiny fraction of the original forest cover remains within its range. Even worse, this small range is located in an area of dense human habitation.

BRAZIL

SNOW LEOPARD
Panthera uncia

SNOW LEOPARDS DO NOT ROAR LIKE OTHER BIG CATS. THEY DO PRODUCE A LOUD MOANING SOUND, BUT THIS IS ONLY USED IN FINDING A MATE.

Native peoples of the Himalayas kill snow leopards because they consider them as predators of domestic livestock and because their fur brings a high price. Reports show that although they are protected in China, snow leopards continue to be hunted and their skin sold on the open market.

A graceful, agile and solitary hunter, the snow leopard can weigh as much as 165 pounds (75 kg), with an average length of almost four feet (120 cm), and a tail averaging three feet (90 cm) long. The snow leopard's light colored fur is patterned by striking black rings and circles.

Found in the high mountains of Central Asia, snow leopards live on a varied diet consisting of mountain goats and sheep, deer, boar, domestic livestock and marmots. Snow leopards usually stalk their prey and leap on it from a distance, occasionally as far away as 50 feet (45 meters) in a single bound. In the summer, snow leopards find their food in alpine meadows and rocky areas, and in winter they may follow their prey down into forested areas.

Breeding occurs early in the year and the young are born from April to June. The litter, usually two or three, is protected in a rocky shelter lined with the mother's fur. The babies stay with the mother through their first winter so they can learn to hunt. Full maturity is attained after two years.

Snow leopards are classified as endangered by the United States Department of the Interior (USDI). They also are on the International Union for Conservation of Nature (IUCN) endangered list and trade is restricted by the Convention on International Trade in Endangered Species (CITES). Despite this, snow leopard numbers continue to decline rapidly. A 1979 report said only 150-300 snow leopards remained in Nepal and a 1988 report estimated roughly 3000 to 10,000 snow leopards remained in the wild throughout their range. (About 400 individuals are held in captivity.)

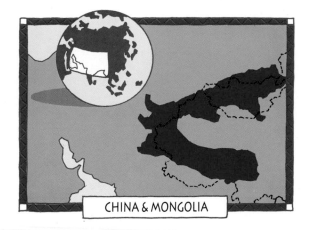

CHINA & MONGOLIA

Rodney Jackson is one of the people that I credit for encouraging me to begin painting wildlife. He is a biologist who has spent many years in Nepal radio collaring & studying the magnificent snow leopard. This gouache painting was modeled from one of Rodney's beautiful photographs. — L.R.

L. Regan © 91

SNOWY EGRET
Egretta thula

THE SNOWY EGRET (ALSO KNOWN AS BREWSTER'S EGRET AND THE LITTLE WHITE HERON) HAS BEEN TIMED IN FLIGHT AT SPEEDS OF UP TO 30 MILES (48 KM) PER HOUR.

The snowy egret, a member of the heron family, is one of the daintiest and most exquisite of all marsh birds. Their feathers were in great demand by plume hunters in the early twentieth century and snowy egrets (along with great egrets) were killed in great numbers to acquire the feathers. Snowy egret feathers are not as stiff as those of the great egret, and were therefore more desirable for hats and garments. Snowy egrets also were more abundant and less elusive than great egrets, making it easier for hunters to kill them. Although snowy egret populations have made a comeback due to rigid preservation efforts, the birds are still considered rare and need special protection in some parts of the United States.

The snowy egret, while similarly plumed in white, is smaller than the great egret. The snowy egret grows to 27 inches (69 cm) long with a 38 inch (97 cm) wingspan. Their wing stroke is quicker than the great egret and the snowy egret is considered a more active bird. Elegant "nuptial plumes," (long, lacy, ribbon-like feathers), adorn the head and neck during mating season.

The snowy egret lives around freshwater, brackish-water and saltwater marshes and swamps. When feeding they use one of their feet while walking to stir the bottom of ponds, or shake marsh plants to expose a meal. Snowy egrets feed on small fish, frogs, lizards, snakes, shrimp, fiddler crabs, crayfish and aquatic insects. Another method used for catching prey is to hover over the water and dive down, scooping up fish in their large bills. Other times, they will run swiftly through the shallows of a pond with wings partly raised to flush their prey.

During mating season snowy egrets perform courting displays attracting their mates with their nuptial plumes. A pair will build a nest either on the ground or high in the trees. They are a social species, nesting in colonies of thousands of pairs along with other herons, egrets and shore birds. Snowy egrets lay between three and five eggs which are incubated by both parents for eighteen days. The young will leave the nest less than four weeks after hatching.

More information is still needed about snowy egrets in order to help the species survive. Preserving their habitats globally and setting aside nesting sites will help ensure these beautiful birds a place to flourish.

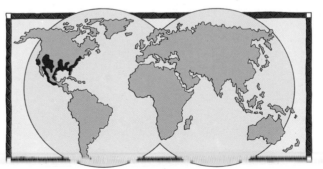

Range: Adjacent to aquatic environments in North America.

MANDRILL
Mandrillus sphinx

TO INTIMIDATE AN INTRUDER, A MANDRILL WILL DISPLAY ABRUPT UP AND DOWN MOVEMENTS OF THE HEAD AND NECK, AND GLARE WITH ITS EYES WHILE KEEPING ITS MOUTH TIGHTLY CLOSED.

As rain forests are destroyed, the mandrill's world grows smaller and less abundant, thereby threatening the extinction of this intriguing primate species. Besides habitat loss, mandrill populations are declining because of excessive hunting.

Mandrills are the largest of all monkeys, the males reaching a shoulder height of twenty inches (50 cm) and weighing up to 120 pounds (54 kg). Found in thick rain forests, mountain forests and on plantations, mandrills forage the ground for food by overturning stones and debris in search of insects, mushrooms and plants. They also eat fruits, nuts and small vertebrates.

Mandrills are most widely recognized for their interesting facial structure and vivid coloring. The prominent nasal bone of the mandrill has grooves and ridges on each side. In the adult male, these grooves and ridges are colored purple, blue and scarlet. While females also have brilliant markings, they lack the males' purple and blue colors.

Mandrills live in "harem" groups: one large adult male and several females plus their young. During the dry season, six or seven such harems will gather to form a troop of 200 or more individuals. Males without a harem will live alone until they have the opportunity to form one.

Mandrills are on the United States Department of the Interior's (USDI) list of endangered animals, and they are listed as vulnerable by the International Union for Conservation of Nature (IUCN). Preservation of African rain forests and other mandrill habitats are needed to help save this species.

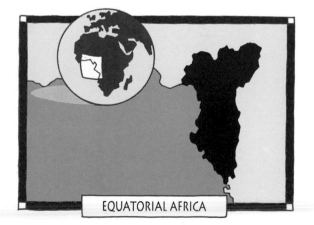

EQUATORIAL AFRICA

MANDRIL   RUFFED LEMUR   PATAS MONKEY

RUFFED LEMUR
Varecia variegata

See illustration on page 41

RUFFED LEMURS LIKE TO SUN-BATHE IN THE EARLY MORNING. SITTING IN A SUNNY SPOT, THEY WILL SPREAD OPEN THEIR ARMS AND LEGS FOR MAXIMUM SOLAR EXPOSURE.

Ruffed lemurs share the Indian Ocean island of Madagascar with a variety of rare flora and fauna. Many species native to Madagascar are found nowhere else on earth and most of them, including the ruffed lemur, are endangered because the forests of this small, biologically diverse island are rapidly being cleared for farmland.

Lemurs are the earliest evolved of the living primates. No larger than a domestic cat, the ruffed lemur is a monkey-like animal with a long, furry tail. They have pointed faces with nostrils at the tip of the snout and distinctive hooked claws in place of their second toes. Black and white ruffed lemurs have black and white fur patterns, no two of which look exactly alike. Red ruffed lemurs are mostly a deep rust red with color patterns which are much more uniform between individuals.

Ruffed lemurs live mostly in trees. They are agile climbers and can leap in great bounds across tree branches. (These skills are quite useful when gathering food.) At dusk and dawn, they travel through the forests in search of fruits, leaves and tree bark.

During a gestation period of between 90 and 102 days, female ruffed lemurs usually make a nest in the hole of a tree, lining it with fur pulled out of their flanks or thighs. While up to six offspring may be born in a litter, two or three is most common, especially with first-time mothers. More than half of the births, which occur in October and November, are of twins. The young are initially carried, kitten-like, by the female and are deposited in a safe, convenient location while she forages nearby. By four or five weeks, young lemurs play actively near the nest and are able to climb to the tops of trees.

Conservation efforts are underway in Madagascar to help save the lemur and many other of the island's rare species, but the problems encountered are complex. For example, it is against the religious beliefs of the native Malagasy people to immediately reuse farmland. Therefore, it is not a matter of bringing new farming techniques to the inhabitants, but of learning about their cultural beliefs to find ways to make compromises that safeguard the island's environment.

Ruffed lemurs are listed as endangered by the United States Department of the Interior (USDI), are considered threatened by the International Union for Conservation of Nature (IUCN), and are protected by the Convention on International Trade in Endangered Species (CITES).

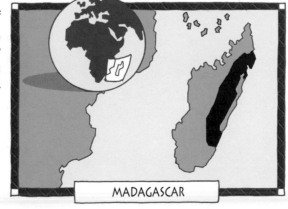

MADAGASCAR

See illustration on page 41

PATAS MONKEY
Erythrocebus patas

The patas monkey inhabits the grass and woodland savannahs of Africa in the region from Senegal, east to Ethiopia and south to Tanzania. As these savannahs are turned into farms, patas monkeys are squeezed out. They are threatened by hunters who kill them for their meat and farmers who kill them for damaging crops.

Unlike most monkeys, this species prefers traveling by ground. They are thought to be the fastest of all primates and have been clocked running at speeds of 34 miles (55 km) per hour.

Usually reddish in color, patas monkeys are 24 to 35 inches (60-87.5 cm) long, with a 20 to 30 inch (51-76 cm) tail. The sexes are dimorphic with the adult male weighing between 15 and 29 pounds (7-13 kg) being much larger than the adult female which weighs between 9 and 15 pounds (4-7 kg).

The bulk of their diet consists of grasses, berries, fruits, beans, seeds, leaves and roots. Occasionally, they will eat mushrooms, insects, lizards and bird eggs.

Patas monkeys wander widely in groups of from ten to thirty individuals, referred to as a troop. Each troop consists of one dominant male plus a hierarchical arrangement of several families and their young. In their daily search for food, the troop will sometimes travel as far as 7.5 miles (12 km). When the troop is eating, the adult male stands on his hind legs and carefully watches for predators such as cheetahs, leopards, hyenas or hunting dogs.

Breeding season occurs between December and February. A single offspring is born after a gestation period of 170 days. After two weeks, the baby begins to explore its surroundings but continues to be carried by its mother for another three months.

Currently, the patas monkey is not listed as either threatened or endangered, but as its habitat vanishes, so too will the chance for this species to thrive. Efforts to save the grasslands and savannahs in regions where the patas monkeys live will help preserve this species.

> PATAS MONKEYS HAVE MANY VOCALIZATIONS, INCLUDING A "BARK," BUT MOST OF THEIR SOUNDS ARE MUTED AND CAN BE HEARD BY HUMANS ONLY WITHIN 110 YARDS (100 METERS).

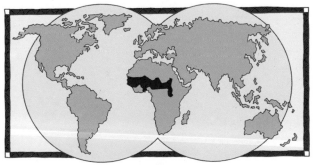

Range: Central Africa from Senegal eastward to Ethiopia, and south to Tanzania.

RED-EYED TREE FROG

Agalychnis callidryas

TREE FROGS ARE ABLE TO JUMP 17 TIMES THEIR OWN BODY LENGTH. IN HUMAN TERMS, THAT WOULD CORRESPOND TO A STANDING BROAD JUMP OF MORE THAN 100 FEET (30 METERS).

The exotic-looking red-eyed tree frog dwells in tropical rainforests from central Mexico to Guatemala. Its peculiar appearance makes it the most sought after of the eight species of tree frogs imported into the United States. While importation alone is a major threat to this species, the red-eyed tree frog also has to contend with its disappearing rainforest habitat.

The red-eyed tree frog's startling colored eyes are accented by vertical pupils, creating an alien-like appearance. The eyes are further emphasized by the frog's contrasting bright green skin which changes to a cream color on its sides and underbelly. The toes are long with soft, round ends, which act as adhesive pads for gripping. Despite their striking features, red-eyed tree frogs are small, reaching only 2.75 inches (7 cm) in length.

Adult red-eyed tree frogs live in the canopy of trees and often spend the daytime hours resting in bromeliads (tropical flowers which cup small amounts of water) or on green leaves. They become active at night hopping in short, quick spurts as they look for insects to eat.

When breeding, red-eyed tree frogs strategically deposit their eggs on a leaf over a small water source, so that when the eggs hatch, the larvae fall directly into the water below where the tadpoles will grow and later metamorphose into frogs. The female may lay three to five clutches of eggs in one night. She produces a jelly from fluids in her bladder with which the eggs are covered. This jelly keeps them from drying and protects them from predators. Hatching occurs about five days after the eggs are laid and metamorphosis takes place 79 days after hatching.

Currently, red-eyed tree frogs are only in moderate danger of extinction. However, since they thrive in rainforest habitats which are seriously threatened by human destruction their numbers will decline as their habitat diminishes.

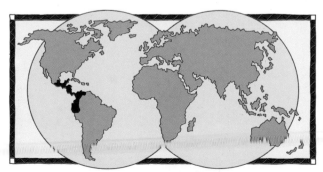

Range: Central America to Equador.

RESPLENDENT QUETZAL
Pharomachrus mocinno

IN PRE-COLUMBIAN TIMES, ROYALTY AND NOBILITY WORE ELABORATE HEADDRESSES OF RESPLENDENT QUETZAL TAIL FEATHERS. THE BIRDS WERE RELEASED AFTER THEIR FEATHERS WERE TAKEN SO THEY COULD GROW NEW FEATHERS AND CONTINUE TO REPRODUCE.

Brilliant colors and long, flowing tail feathers give the resplendent quetzal a breathtaking appearance which, arguably, makes it the most gorgeous bird in the world. The quetzal is the national bird of Guatemala where it is enshrined on public buildings and honored on postage stamps. Even Guatemalan money is named after the quetzal. For centuries in Central America the resplendent quetzal has been hunted for its exquisite tail feathers. When the first systematic naming of the world's plants and animals began in the eighteenth century, the resplendent quetzal was not included, apparently because it was already so rare as to be considered mythological.

The word resplendent means "shining brilliantly," and the quetzal could not have been more aptly named. Magnificent feathers of iridescent green and bright blue cover its body. The underbelly is deep crimson and the tail is a lovely white. More vivid green feathers, which sometimes reach a length of three feet (90 cm), extend beyond the end of the white tail feathers.

Resplendent quetzals live in the misty cloud forests that exist in the mountains stretching from southern Mexico to western Panama. Ranging from an altitude of 4,000 to 10,000 feet (1,212 to 3,030 meters), the cloud forests are in a constant mist of rainfall throughout the year. This environment provides the resplendent quetzal a diet of lush fruits, especially those from the laurel and avocado families, a myriad of insects, snails, spiders, frogs and lizards which they also eat.

During the mating season, the male resplendent quetzal performs a display flight in which he flies high above the forest canopy making circles, then drops back into the foliage and gives a distinctive "wac-wac" call. A mated pair will nest in a rotting tree trunk where two eggs are laid on a nest of loose fragments of wood. Both sexes incubate the eggs for 17 to 19 days. After hatching, young resplendent quetzals are fed insects until they are ready to leave the nest (in about twenty-nine days).

Resplendent quetzals currently are protected by the International Union for Conservation of Nature (IUCN). Trade or hunting of the quetzal is prohibited by the Convention on International Trade in Endangered Species (CITES). The almost total destruction of the original forest over the central valley of Costa Rica and nearly all the central highlands of Guatemala is responsible for the disappearance of the quetzal from these regions. Further destruction of Central American forests must cease if the resplendent quetzal is to remain more than just a myth.

CENTRAL AMERICA

GREEN IGUANA
Iguana iguana

GREEN IGUANAS ARE ECTO-THERMIC (COLD BLOODED), MEANING THEY DO NOT KEEP A CONSTANT BODY TEMPERA-TURE. INSTEAD, THEIR BODY TEMPERATURE IS DETERMINED BY THE ENVIRONMENT.

While the green iguana faces considerable peril from habitat destruction, this unusual-looking reptile also faces other problems that threaten extinction. Often called "chicken of the trees," iguanas are considered a valuable food source by some native peoples. Their eggs are boiled in salt water and sold as a delicacy. Green iguanas are also a popular bait for catching crocodilians. In addition, green iguanas are in high demand by the pet industry.

With scaly bodies and four well-developed legs, green iguanas grow to as long as 6.7 feet (204 cm) of which two-thirds are their long, spiny tails. Male green iguanas have a dorsal crest of prickly spines three-inches (8 cm) high. Both males and females have a flap of skin under the chin called a "dewlap," which is important in visual displays.

Adult green iguanas are vegetarians. They feed primarily on leafy plants, but especially favor the wild plum and other types of fruits. While they are generally herbaceous, young green iguanas have been known to feed on insects and small animals.

Green iguanas live in trees, choosing high branches near or over water for resting places. If they are frightened, they will jump, from as high as 20 feet (6 meters), to the ground or dive into the water where they can swim submerged for several minutes. During cool or rainy weather they move to the ground.

Mating and nesting occurs in the dry season. A female green iguana digs a six foot (183 cm) deep by twelve inch (30.5 cm) wide burrow (a process that takes her two days). She lays an average of 30 eggs in the nest and fills it with soil and plant debris. Afterwards, she makes "mock burrows" near the real one to conceal the location of the actual nest. Young iguanas hatch about two months later, during the rainy season.

Green iguanas are protected by the Convention on International Trade in Endangered Species (CITES). Current conservation efforts to save tropical forests also benefit the green iguana. However, public education and awareness programs must also be established concerning the pet trade and native hunting to prevent further depletion of iguana populations.

Range: Tropical regions of Central and South America plus the Lesser Antilles.

This is actually the jacket painting for the book "Welcome to the Green House" that I illustrated for Jane Yolen. We wanted something that would be eye-catching, but would still work well with all the lettering that has to go on the cover. I thought this iguana had a lot of personality & the macaw had wonderful color. It's so important to stress that in destroying our Rain Forests we are not just burning down trees; we are killing millions of beautiful creatures. — L.R.

JAGUAR
Panthera onca

THE JAGUAR POPULATION ACTUALLY INCREASED IN COLONIAL TIMES WHEN LIVESTOCK WAS BROUGHT TO THE SAVANNAHS OF SOUTH AMERICA, AN AREA PREVIOUSLY LACKING IN NATURAL PREY FOR THE JAGUAR.

Just as the fur of leopards and other spotted cats were in demand for fur trade in the 1960s, there was also a great increase in the demand for jaguar skins. Some estimates show that 15,000 jaguars were killed annually during that time in the Amazon region of Brazil alone. Currently, loss of habitat plus elimination for killing livestock are taking their toll on this exotic species.

Sometimes this new world cat is confused with the old world leopard in appearance, however, the jaguar is much larger and has a shorter tail. Another way to tell them apart is by their spots. The jaguar has spots inside its spots and the leopard does not. Male jaguars are larger than the females, their weights varying from 80 to 350 pounds (36 to 159 kg). They can grow to six feet (185 cm) in length, but their tails usually only get about 2.5 feet (75 cm) long. Jaguars are good climbers, spending much of their time in trees. They are excellent swimmers as well.

Jaguars hunt in forests and savannahs at night. They stalk or ambush their prey and drag it to a sheltered spot for eating. Their favorite catches are peccaries, capybaras, tapirs, crocodilians and fish.

Jaguars are basically solitary, territorial animals. They are much like cougars or tigers in that the females have home ranges which overlap one another, while resident males use areas twice as large which encompass the range of several females. Female jaguars carry their young for three months and deliver one to four babies. They den in caves, canyons or ruins of old buildings, where the young will stay with their mothers for nearly two years.

By the early twentieth century, most jaguar populations had disappeared from the United States. The jaguar is classified as endangered by the United States, vulnerable by the International Union for the Conservation of Nature (IUCN) and is protected by the Convention on International Trade in Endangered Species (CITES). National and international conservation measures seem to have reduced the killing of jaguars, but illegal trade in skins must be stopped and strong habitat protection programs must be established to permanently save this endangered species.

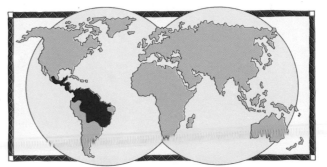

Range: Mexico to central Patagonia.

CAPUCHIN MONKEY/WHITE-FACED SAPAJOU

Cebus capucinus

IN COASTAL AREAS WHERE WHITE-FACED SAPAJOUS ARE NOT HUNTED OR HARASSED, THEY ARE KNOWN TO TRAVEL IN GROUPS THAT MAKE BOLD DISPLAYS AT HUMANS WHEN THREATENED.

There are four species of capuchin monkeys, also called "ringtail" monkeys due to their habit of carrying their tails in a coiled position. These intelligent and active monkeys were favored as pets in the United States and Europe. The capuchin is the monkey we see dressed in a little red suit and used for entertainment by the traditional organ grinder. While they can adapt to captivity, they are obviously best suited to life in the wild.

The white-faced sapajou is the most interestingly colored of all the capuchin monkeys. Its body and tail are predominantly black and white, while its face and throat tend to be white. As with all capuchins, it has a somewhat prehensile (grasping) tail which is used like an additional hand. The tail is naked at the tip and is soft underneath. White-faced sapajous use their tails to brace or steady themselves. Its sensitive tip is also used for touching.

White-faced sapajous live in a variety of forests in Central America and northwestern South America. They eat a varied diet consisting of fruits, nuts, berries, seeds, flowers, buds, shoots, bark, gums, insects, eggs, and infrequently, small vertebrates and certain kinds of marine life gathered at low tide, such as oysters and crabs.

White-faced sapajous live in groups, dominated by an adult male, which range in size from six to fifty individuals. There are generally more females than males in a group. A female gives birth to a single baby, which immediately clings tightly with both hands and feet to its mother's hair. As the baby gets stronger, it will climb about on its mother or play nearby. If a young monkey becomes separated from its mother, other members of the troop will respond to its distress cries. Full size and sexual maturity are reached by females at about four years of age and by males at about eight years.

While the white-faced sapajou and other capuchin monkeys are still somewhat abundant, many of their relatives are vulnerable to extinction due to widespread habitat loss and hunting. Researchers have noted that the opportunity to observe and understand capuchin monkeys in the wild may soon be gone because of the destruction of the rainforests. It is now illegal to import capuchin monkeys into the United States for pets or entertainment purposes.

CENTRAL & S. AMERICA

WEST AFRICAN CROWNED CRANE

Balearica pavonina

THEIR MOST ELABORATE DISPLAYS ARE DURING MATING, WHEN THEY GRACEFULLY PERFORM THEIR BEAUTIFUL "NUPTIAL DANCE," AND DURING FIGHTING WHEN THEY AGGRESSIVELY KICK AND STAB WITH THEIR BEAKS.

While the West African crowned crane is common in captivity, its numbers are declining in the wild. Construction of dams within its habitat has caused the destruction of wetlands where it lives. Furthermore, since cranes are showy, colorful birds, they are popular zoo animals and have become a favorite "item" for private collectors as well. Chicks are captured by private collectors before they can fly and often die from inadequate care.

West African crowned cranes are tall birds, reaching a height of more than three feet (91-102 cm). The bodies and necks are slate-grey. Their wings are black and white. Their foreheads have feathers of velvety black that contrast with the stiff straw-colored plumage of their ornate "crowns."

Crowned cranes stamp their feet while walking through grassy vegetation, apparently to expose or flush out insects and small lizards. In addition, they eat a variety of plants, including maize, bean pods and flower heads.

Mating is a spectacular event where they perform an elaborate courtship ritual called the "nuptial dance." This "dance" is an exhibit of graceful leaps, rhythmic head-dips, bobbing motions and circular movements. Towards the end of the performance, one bird finally tires, at which time they will rest and afterwards fly off together. The pair forms a long-term bond, where mutual preening and display behavior is common.

Both members of the pair share nest building responsibilities. The nest is made by trampling marsh vegetation into a circular area 16 to 50 feet (5 to 15 meters) in diameter. The female lays two to three eggs and both parents help in the 30 day incubation period. Within 24 hours of hatching, crowned crane chicks are venturing out of the nest in search of food. Nine or ten months later the parents are ready to nest again at which time the fully-grown offspring are driven away.

West African crowned cranes are one of the fifteen different species of cranes in the world. The International Crane Foundation (ICF), located in Baraboo, Wisconsin, is a refuge for all fifteen species. The ICF is dedicated to the preservation of cranes and their habitat through captive breeding, research, reintroduction, education and habitat protection. Seven of the fifteen crane species are on the endangered list, the other eight are endangered in specific locations within their ranges.

Range: South of the Sahara and north of the Congo Basin in west central Africa.

MOOSE

Alces alces

THE MAXIMUM RECORDED ANTLER SPREAD OF A MOOSE IS 6.75 FEET (206 CM).

By early 1900 the moose population in the contiguous United States was nearly wiped out. Uncontrolled hunting for moose meat, leather and bone was the cause of the near extinction of this species. Subsequent protection and management measures allowed the moose to rebuild its numbers in some regions. Small populations have returned to New England, the upper Great Lakes region and the central Rocky Mountains.

Easily identified by its broad overhanging muzzle and large spatulated antlers, the moose can grow to a shoulder height of almost eight feet (244 cm). With a heavy mane and a characteristic pendulous flap of skin beneath the throat, (known as the "bell"), the moose is the largest member of the deer family.

Moose roam carefully and quietly through the underbrush in wooded areas, preferring a moist habitat where willows and poplars are abundant. They forage in marshy and timbered regions using shrubs and trees for browse, and will feed on water vege-tation eating the roots and stems of lake bottom plants. In the winter, moose eat twigs, the bark of trees and small plants they find by pawing through the snow.

Although they are solitary animals, many moose may gather in a small area where food is abundant during late fall or winter. In the breeding season, several males compete for a single female, engaging in elaborate displays and shoving matches using their antlers. Mating occurs in the fall with birth occurring in the spring. A single calf, occasionally two, is born each year. The calf stays with its mother for the following year until she chases it away after giving birth to another calf.

Now that conservation efforts are being made on behalf of this valued species, each moose has an increased chance of living its full life span of about 27 years. This results in more reproductive years for each individual and the likelihood of continued population growth for the species.

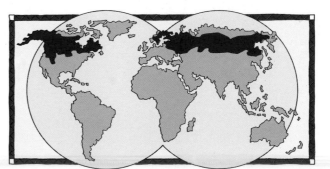

Range: Northern North America, Scandinavia and Northern Asia.

Snowshoe Hare
Lepus americanus

SNOWSHOE HARES EXTRACT THE MAXIMUM VALUE FROM THEIR AVAILABLE FOOD BY EXPELLING MOIST PELLETS WHICH ARE LATER EATEN SO THAT THE FOOD TRAVELS THROUGH THE DIGESTIVE TRACT TWICE.

The snowshoe hare experiences unique cyclical fluctuations in its population. This cycle begins when snowshoe hares are too abundant and deplete their food source. Once the population decreases and vegetation has time to recover, these hares increase in number until their population is again too large to be supported by their environment. Because the snowshoe hare is a major food source for birds of prey and other predators, such as the lynx (*Felis lynx*), when snowshoe hare populations decline, so do predator populations.

People commonly mistake snowshoe hares for rabbits. Although both hares and rabbits are closely related, there are physical distinctions between the two. The skull structure is different, hares have longer ears which are black-tipped, and they are larger overall than rabbits. Also, young hares are more developed when born.

The snowshoe hare, sometimes called the "varying hare," has a seasonal change in its coat (pelage). In the winter, they molt from brown to white, which makes them less conspicuous in snow. However, an early snowfall can catch a snowshoe hare on a white landscape with its pelage still brown.

During the day, snowshoe hares will seek shelter under a bush, log or stump in a forested area. They are most active at night, feeding mainly on grasses and tender vegetation. When they have overgrazed the area, or in places where grasses are not available, they will eat buds, twigs and bark.

Snowshoe hares do not live in burrows, rather they depend on their strong running abilities to escape danger. They use a complex system of runways that they have cleared through the grass and undergrowth for easy getaways. In winter, they pack the snow down to form these escape routes.

Breeding takes place from mid-March to September. The gestation period for snowshoe hares is 36 days. They may have up to four litters each year. Usually four young (called leverets) are born in each litter, but during periods of rapid population growth, litter size can more than double.

Leverets are born with fur and open eyes. They can move about in a relatively short time. (In contrast, young rabbits are born helpless.) The young are concealed in dense vegetation where their mother visits for a brief period at dusk to nurse them.

A species of hare in Florida, the lower keys marsh rabbit (*Sylvilagus palustris herneri*), is classified as endangered, and some populations of snowshoe hares are threatened as their forest habitats are cleared. While hares are not in immediate danger of extinction, they are a valuable food source for other threatened species. Declining snowshoe hare populations could affect not only this species but also its rare predators.

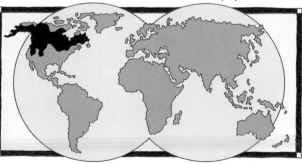

Range: Alaska, Canada, and northern parts of the United States.

L.Regan

OCELOT
Felis pardalis

ONE SUBSPECIES OF OCELOT (F. P. ALBESCENS), WHICH ONCE ROAMED OVER MOST OF TEXAS AND AS FAR EAST AS ARKANSAS AND LOUISIANA, IS NOW THOUGHT TO HAVE A POPULATION OF LESS THAN 1,000.

The ocelot still roams over most of its original range but its numbers are declining because of habitat loss and hunting. Prior to 1972 when importation into the United States was prohibited, enormous numbers of ocelot skins were brought into this country. (A reported 133,069 furs were imported in 1969.)

While the ocelot's size varies considerably from that of a large domestic cat to a small leopard, their average length is 30 inches (76 cm) with a 15 inch (38 cm) tail. They also vary in color from a dark olive-gray with black spots to a creamy-yellow with spots of rust and black. They typically weigh about 22 to 26 pounds (10-12 kg).

Generally nocturnal, ocelots sleep by day in hollow trees or on branches. They roam a great variety of habitats from humid tropical forests to fairly dry scrub country. They are excellent climbers, jumpers and swimmers. Consequently, they are able to catch a variety of food, including fish, snakes, birds, rabbits and rodents.

Ocelots communicate by mewing, and during courtship by yowls, not unlike those of a domestic cat. They like to travel alone but they make frequent contact with other ocelots. Breeding usually produces one or two young after a normal gestation period of 79 to 82 days.

Classified as endangered by the United States Department of the Interior (USDI), ocelots also are protected by the laws of most countries in which they live. They are listed as vulnerable by the International Union for Conservation of Nature (IUCN), and trade is restricted by the Convention on International Trade in Endangered Species (CITES).

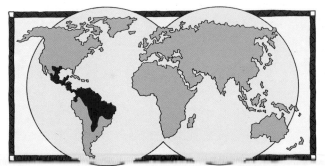

Range: Southwestern United States to northern Argentina.

This ocelot belonged to a dear artist friend of mine who was living in Panama at the time. He furnished me with many wonderful photographs that I was able to use as illustrations for a children's book about the Rain Forest. I wanted this beautiful cat to look alert, but not too threatening. — L.R.

GREAT EGRET
Casmerodius albus

THE GREAT EGRET ALSO IS KNOWN BY SEVERAL OTHER NAMES INCLUDING AMERICAN EGRET, COMMON EGRET, LARGE EGRET, WHITE EGRET, AND GREAT WHITE HERON.

It is estimated that during a single year in the late nineteenth century, 200,000 great egrets were killed for their plumage which was used to decorate women's hats and other garments. The Royal Society for the Protection of Birds in Britain and the Audubon Society in America were originally formed to help protect the great egret from this threat. Today, the chief danger facing this species is wetland drainage and destruction.

Great egrets are known for their splendid head and neck "capes" or "nuptial trains," of flowing white feathers. They grow this delicate array of plumes, which are used in courtship displays, in the winter and shed the entire cape in summer. Great egrets are tall birds with long, slender legs and a slim elongated neck. They have a wingspan of 55 inches (140 cm) and are 37 to 41 inches (94-104 cm) long in the body. Male and female egrets look alike, except that males are slightly larger.

Great egrets commonly feed in salt- and freshwater marshes and ponds. They eat fish, frogs, salamanders, snakes, crayfish, mice and aquatic insects.

Great egrets nest both singly or in colonies in trees near the water's edge. Each male establishes a small territory around his chosen nest site, then he builds a platform of twigs or reeds on which he performs a showy display to attract a female. Once a mate has been secured, both sexes work together to finish the nest. The female then lays from three to five eggs which are incubated for 24 days until hatched. Six weeks after hatching, the young egrets are ready to fly.

The destruction of marshes and swamps is a critical threat to these graceful birds. As humans drain wetlands for development, great egret populations decline. Conservation efforts must be increased in the United States, Canada and abroad to save this habitat since wetlands are the only environment in which great egrets can feed.

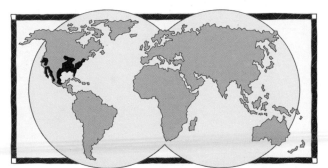

Range: United States in most fresh- and saltwater coastal locations.

ANCIENT INDIANS AND ESKIMOS THOUGHT THE WOLF SYMBOLIZED RETURNING SPIRITS.

For some time conservationists have been trying to dispel the ancient myths of the "evil" wolf and present a truer picture of its behavior. Our human fear of wolves has resulted in an all-out war waged against this animal using traps, poisons, guns and specially trained dogs. In addition, loss of habitat, parasitic heartworm and the deadly disease, canine parvovirus (spread by domestic dogs), threaten this species.

Strong and beautiful, gray wolves are the largest member of the dog family. (Wolves are the ancestors of domestic dogs.) Their thick gray fur, patterned with white and silver streaks, is the most striking feature of this majestic animal. Keen eyes allow wolves to be active at night and enable them to find their way through the long tunnels that lead to their dens.

Wolves are highly social animals. They form packs for protection and for overcoming prey up to 10 times their own size. A mated pair usually stays together for life. The packs, which are hostile toward one another, are formed around a mated pair and their offspring from the previous two years. The alpha, or dominant, male leads the pack.

In wilderness areas, wolves typically prey upon moose, deer and caribou. However, smaller animals such as hares, beavers and rodents are an important part of their diet. When living near humans, they will kill domestic livestock and forage through trash. These practices have escalated the war between the wolves and humans.

While wolves have been eliminated throughout large portions of their range, populations remain in various parts of the northern hemisphere. The wolf is in danger of extinction within the continental United States because of the conflict between wolves and humans. Controversy has raged for years over the need to reintroduce the wolf into areas such as Yellowstone National Park. Ranchers and farmers feel threatened by wolves because of attacks on livestock.

While programs have been set up to pay ranchers for their losses to wolves, controversy surrounding gray wolf protection continues. Although the wolf is classified as endangered, permits can be obtained for killing wolves that prey on livestock. The International Union for the Conservation of Nature (IUCN) classifies the wolf as vulnerable, and the species is protected by the Convention on International Trade in Endangered Species (CITES).

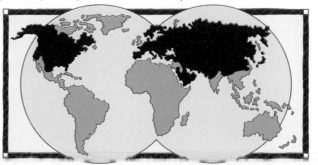

Range: North America, Europe, Asia, and the Middle East.

POLAR BEAR
Ursus maritimus

DUE TO THEIR BODY FAT AND BECAUSE THE OUTER HAIR FOLLICLES OF THEIR FUR ARE HOLLOW, POLAR BEARS ARE BUOYANT, SWIMMING RATHER HIGH WITH THEIR HEADS AND SHOULDERS ABOVE THE WATER.

Native peoples of the Arctic have long hunted the polar bear for its fat and fur. Sport and commercial hunting increased in Alaska during the late 1940s when aircraft were used to locate polar bears. Currently, polar bears are facing an even greater threat since the limited areas suitable for denning by pregnant females are being damaged by oil and gas activity in the Arctic.

With a thick coat of snowy-white fur and large insulated feet, a polar bear is well suited for a cold, icy environment. Classified with marine mammals, polar bears have forefeet which are oar-like in shape for greater mobility in the water. While their fur may turn yellow from the sun in the summer, once they shed it is again pure white. (It can also appear yellow at times by the way light reflects off the hair follicles.)

Adult polar bears can reach a length of more than eight feet (244 cm) with a shoulder height of 5.25 feet (160 cm). Females can weigh as much as 660 pounds (299 kg) with males sometimes reaching a hefty 1,764 pounds (800 kg).

These large bears prefer a habitat of pack ice that is subject to periodic fracturing by wind and sea currents. The refreezing of such fractures produces thinner ice where hunting is most successful. Polar bears feed primarily on the ringed seal (*Phoca hispida*). They catch seals by remaining very still until the seal emerges from the water, or by stalking hauled out

seals on the ice. Sometimes the bears will kill young seals by raiding seal dens. Polar bears also eat sea birds, carcasses of stranded marine mammals, small land mammals, reindeer, fish and vegetation. (Berries are a favorite food during summer and autumn.)

Polar bears make a den in the winter for temporary shelter during severe weather. While males do not hibernate, female polar bears that are pregnant hibernate during the winter months. Males and females come together only briefly in the spring during the mating season. Births take place the following winter while the mother is hibernating in her den. Usually two cubs are born, staying with their mother for two years until she is ready to mate again. Polar bears are estimated to live between 25 and 30 years in the wild.

The Polar Bear Specialist Group of the Species Survival Commission of the International Union for Conservation of Nature (IUCN) meets every two years to discuss polar bear research and management on an international basis. In 1972, the killing of polar bears, except by natives for subsistence, was prohibited by the United States Marine Mammal Protection Act. They also are protected by the Convention on International Trade in Endangered Species (CITES). In addition, the Russian Federation, Canada, Denmark and Norway have restricted hunting of polar bears, except for specified groups of natives who depend on polar bears for their survival.

Arctic Ocean

ARCTIC REGION

L Regan '91

LION
Panthera leo

THE ROMANS USED LIONS IMPORTED FROM NORTH AFRICA AND ASIA MINOR AS EXECUTIONERS, A PRACTICE WHICH CONTINUED IN EUROPE UNTIL MEDIEVAL TIMES.

Once called the "king of beasts," the lion is now being overthrown. This species, like many other endangered animals, is faced with a double-edged sword. The animals the lions eat are being depleted as human development increases, yet when they turn to livestock as a source of food, they are considered unwanted predators and are killed.

Male lions are considerably larger than the females, gaining some of their size from their thick, beautiful, brown manes. Their manes are thought to serve as protection for the neck when fighting with other male lions. Females do not have a mane and depend largely on males for protection. Weighing as much as 550 pounds (250 kg), a male lion can reach a shoulder height of four feet (122 cm). Females weigh up to 400 pounds (182 kg), with a shoulder height of 3.5 feet (107 cm).

Female lions do almost all of the hunting. They are not fast runners and therefore most hunts fail. Nonetheless, each lioness may kill as many as 20 large prey each year. To make a successful kill, lions must stalk slowly, alternately creeping and freezing, utilizing every available bit of cover, and then leap for a surprise attack. Hunting in this way, they are able to catch wildebeasts, impalas, giraffes, buffalo, wild hogs, zebras and crocodiles. If these prey are scarce, lions turn to smaller animals and livestock, and occasionally have been known to attack humans.

Lions are the most social of the cats, forming prides of related females and their young. They stay together for years and do not allow strange females to join them. Daughters of group members are recruited into the pride, but young males depart as they approach maturity. Lone male lions or small groups of males will join the pride for variable lengths of time. While a single dominant female rules the pride, male lions are given first priority for eating the kill. Females eat after the males and cubs are often pushed aside with nothing to eat.

Female lions are pregnant for only 100-119 days, a relatively short time for such large animals. Usually three or four very small cubs are born in a litter. Females rear their cubs together and the babies may suckle from any lactating female in the pride. Unfortunately, the survival rate for cubs is low: 80 percent may die before the age of two, in part due to not getting enough to eat.

The trend in lion conservation in Africa is to restrict them to protected areas, parks and reserves. Although this protects lion populations from current threats, fragmentation of the species leads to inbreeding and loss of genetic viability.

The Asiatic lion subspecies is classified as endangered by the United States Department of the Interior (USDI), endangered by the International Union for the Conservation of Nature (IUCN), and trade is restricted by the Convention on International Trade in Endangered Species (CITES).

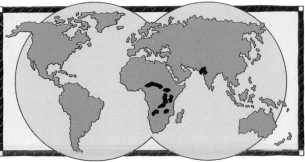

Range: Semidesert areas of Africa and the Gir Forests of western India.

I was in Tanzania, East Africa when I saw this adorable lion cub. I couldn't believe how amazingly close I was able to get to him. We were driving along slowly in our Land Rover when we suddenly came upon a pride of thirteen lions, including a mother carrying a cub by the loose skin on its neck. The lions seemed quite curious & spent a long time sniffing at us & playing with the tires on the Rover. I was able to lean way out my window so that I was only about four feet away from this little guy. It was really a thrill for me, although I think a bit of a concern for our guide! —L.R.

L. Regan © 91

KEEL-BILLED TOUCAN
Ramphastos sulphuratus

THEIR LARGE BILLS DRAG THEM DOWN DURING GLIDING AND THEY MUST FLAP WILDLY TO ASCEND AGAIN, CREATING AN UNGRACEFUL UP AND DOWN FLIGHT PATTERN.

Although all toucans have bright, prominent bills, the keel-billed toucan is the most vibrant bird with its multi-colored beak and yellow breast. Keel-billed toucans live in tropical forests from Mexico to South America. Their livelihood depends on the fragile balance between the many species of flora and fauna that occur naturally in warm forested areas. Human destruction of these forests ruins the delicate balance and risks the survival of many species, including the keel-billed toucan.

Keel-billed toucans have diagonal serrations on the outer edges of their bills which are different from other toucans. They have five colors on their large beaks while other toucans have two or three. Their legs are strong and each foot has two front and two hind toes for solid gripping. Keel-billed toucans are eighteen to twenty-two inches (45-56 cm) long from head to tail.

Keel-billed toucans feed on a wide variety of plants, including catkins, berries and other fruits. They pluck fruit from trees, easily reaching the outer branches

with their long bills. With the food secure in the tip of its beak, the toucan tosses its head backwards, thrusting the fruit into its throat for swallowing. They also use this technique when eating insects, spiders, snakes, lizards and bird eggs.

Normally seen in pairs or small flocks of between six to twelve birds, keel-billed toucans are moderately gregarious. They nest in holes of decaying tree trunks, laying from two to four eggs on a few chips of wood inside the hole. Both parents share incubation for sixteen days. When the helpless nestlings hatch, they are fed bits of fruit and insects by both parents. The young have short colorless bills and are featherless when first born. They slowly develop color in growing their bills and are fully feathered after four weeks. By the seventh week of age, they are ready to fly from the nest.

Keel-billed toucans are protected by the Convention on International Trade in Endangered Species (CITES). Efforts to save tropical forests in Central and South America will help secure a future for this colorful bird.

CENTRAL & S. AMERICA

TOCO TOUCAN
Ramphastos toco

TOCO TOUCANS, LIKE OTHER MEMBERS OF THE TOUCAN FAMILY, ARE PLAYFUL BIRDS AND ENGAGE IN VARIOUS GAMES. ONE GAME IS PLAYED BY TOSSING A PIECE OF FRUIT BACK AND FORTH BETWEEN UP TO AS MANY AS FOUR BIRDS.

The toco toucan is the largest of all toucans. It is also the most widely recognized toucan because its likeness appears on everything from fabrics to paintings to cereal boxes. It has become a symbol of tropical South America.

Considered relatively common within its range, toco toucans are often seen near inhabited areas. The threat to this species is by the destruction of the warm, tropical forests where they meet.

Toco toucans have black and white plumage with massive yellowish-orange bills that are black at the tip. The bill is lightweight and is supported by a system of strong bony layers. Adult toco toucans measure twenty-four inches (61 cm) from head to tail. The beak of the male can reach up to nine inches (23 cm) in length! Female beaks are slightly shorter.

Toco toucans live in trees at the edge of a forest or open woodland. They forage in loose flocks or family groups, flying from tree to tree with the undulating flap/glide characteristic of all larger toucans. They feed mainly on fruit, but they also eat insects and invertebrates, as well as the eggs and young of other birds. To move food from the tip of its long beak a toco toucan flips the food backwards with a jerk of its head, propelling it to the back of its throat for swallowing.

Toco toucans nest in holes of decaying trees, often occupying abandoned woodpecker holes. They favor openings that are barely wide enough to climb through and use the same nesting site for several years in a row. The nest is lined with wood chips covered with an accumulation of regurgitated seeds. Toco toucan parents take turns incubating an average of three eggs for up to sixteen days. Nestlings are born blind and featherless. They are fed tiny morsels of fruit and insects by both parents until they are mature enough (about seven weeks after hatching) to fly from the nest.

To keep the toco toucan from becoming endangered, efforts must be made to stop the destruction of the open woodlands and forests of South America. Although this species is one of the few that can adapt to human encroachment, it is best suited for survival in its natural habitat.

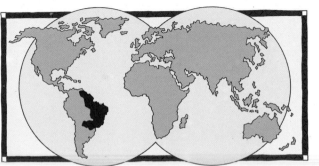

Range: Eastern South America from Guiana to northern Argentina.

CAVE BAT
Myotis velifer

EACH CAVE BAT CAN CATCH UP TO 600 MOSQUITOES IN AN HOUR. LARGE COLONIES OF THESE BATS CONSUME COUNTLESS BILLIONS OF INSECTS EACH SEASON.

It is unfortunate that bats are often perceived in a negative way. Bats are actually important insectivores, pollinators and seed dispersers. They play a vital role in the maintenance of a healthy ecosystem. Many bats are seriously threatened by loss of habitat and by being killed by humans out of fear or ignorance. The cave bat, which lives in the southwestern United States south to Honduras, has declined drastically in the United States from both the disturbance of bat colonies and loss of riverbank habitat along the Colorado River.

The cave bat is a medium-sized bat with a 1¾ inch (4.4 cm) forearm. It is dull brown above and paler below with a woolly-haired appearance.

The cave bat typically roosts in caves and mine tunnels, but hollow trees and man-made structures are also suitable. Within their roosting area they seek crevices or vertical walls and move frequently. While some bats migrate for the winter, others such as the cave bat hibernate.

The cave bat roosts by day and forages at night. Feeding flights usually alternate with periods of rest, during which the bat hangs upside down and digests its meal, which consists mainly of insects. Insects are caught by using "echo-location," the bat's extremely effective sonar system. As the bat flies, it emits through the nose or mouth a series of high frequency sounds (above the limit of human hearing) that bounce back from objects. The bat hears the reflected sound waves which allow it to fly in absolute darkness and detect insect prey.

The cave bat is gregarious and it establishes colonies where great numbers of bats roost together. Mating occurs in fall when the male deposits sperm in the uterus of the female where it is stored during winter hibernation. In early spring ovulation and fertilization occur with births taking place in late spring or early summer. Within the larger colony, the females form maternity colonies to bear young. Most bats normally have a single young. Few, if any, male bats are present after the young are born. Young cave bats can fly after three weeks and sexual maturity is reached by the end of the first year of life.

There is concern for the future of several North American species of brown bats, including the cave bat, due to destruction of cave roosting colonies by humans. They gray bat (Myotis grisescens) and the Indiana bat (Myotis sodalis) are listed as endangered by the United States Department of the Interior (USDI). Both species have declined through such factors as deliberate killing of bats by humans, reckless cave exploration and commercialization of caves for tourism.

Range: Southwestern United States to Honduras.

©1993 U.Regan

MOUNTAIN ZEBRA

Equus zebra

FEMALE ZEBRAS HAVE A FACIAL EXPRESSION CALLED "ESTRUS FACE." THIS EXPRESSION WILL LAST ONLY A FEW SECONDS, BUT IS REPEATED HOURLY OVER A TWO-DAY PERIOD TO LET MALE ZEBRAS KNOW SHE IS READY TO MATE.

Hunting of the mountain zebra in South Africa during the 1930s almost brought this species to extinction. By 1986, half of the existing population of 474 were thought to be living in Mountain Zebra National Park, which was established for their protection.

Striking black and white stripes are the unmistakable trademark of the zebra. Subspecies of zebra are distinguished by the pattern of their stripes and their body size. The mountain zebra is distinctly smaller than the more common zebra, has thicker black stripes and is classified as endangered.

Found on slopes and plateaus in mountainous areas of South Africa, mountain zebras move to lower elevations in the winter. More than half of their daylight hours are spent feeding on a diet consisting mainly of grass and occasionally leaves and bark. Zebras are never far from water since they cannot survive longer than three days without it. They will dig new water holes (up to three feet deep) in river beds if other water holes are dry.

Members of the horse family, mountain zebras herd together in small bands with a single adult stallion as the dominant male. As the leader of several mares and their young, the stallion may keep his group together for as long as 15 years.

Young zebras eventually leave their original band to become a part of their own group. Stallions are capable of establishing herd dominance at the age of five; the females of the herd establish a hierarchy of their own, with one dominant female. Mares start having offspring at age three. A female zebra is pregnant for 12 months before a single baby is born, usually during the rainy season.

When threatened by a predator a zebra herd will gather in close formation. The dominant female leads the band and the stallion takes a defensive position at the rear. If this system does not work, the zebras will defend themselves by kicking out with their hind legs.

Neither the zebras' group formation nor kicking can protect the mountain zebra from the guns of hunters. Conservation programs and education are vital for the survival of this species.

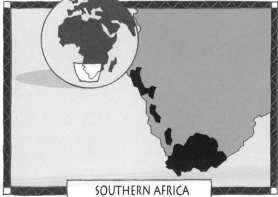

SOUTHERN AFRICA

L.Regan ©1990

Sometimes I paint animals with very unlikely backdrops. Often it's because the patterns & colors work well together, but I just had fun with this one. I could almost hear an imaginary voice saying "Marge, those darn zebras are in the peony bushes again!" — L.R.

COLLARED PECCARY
Tayassu tajacu

COLLARED PECCARIES WALLOW IN THE MUD, BUT THIS PRACTICE, AND THEIR HABIT OF PAWING SAND AGAINST THEIR BELLIES, ARE ACTUALLY CLEANING ACTIVITIES.

While collared peccary populations decline in some areas of its range, other areas show a growth in numbers. This pig-like creature suffers from the extensive Latin American hide trade. In this region, the collared peccary also is killed for food. By contrast, since the time of the early European explorers, the collared peccary has extended its range into the southwestern United States. In this area, it is classified as a game animal and regulated sport hunting is permitted.

The collared peccary and the closely related white-lipped peccary (*Tayassu pecari*), are also known as "javelinas." This is the Spanish word for javelin or spear, which refers to their sharp tusks. Collared peccaries are a dark greenish black color with a "collar" of yellow hair. They are two and one half to three feet (76-91 cm) long with a short, two-inch (5 cm) tail. Collared peccaries reach a shoulder height of nearly two feet (61 cm) and weigh up to 66 pounds (30 kg).

Collared peccaries frequent water holes and, like pigs, wallow in mud and dust. They have poor vision and fair hearing so they depend on their sense of smell when foraging for food. They "grub" with their snouts for tubers, bulbs, nuts and cactus fruit. They

also consume grubs, bird eggs, snakes and small vertebrates.

The collared peccary is communal, living in groups of up to fifty individuals of both sexes and all ages. In most of its range, breeding occurs throughout the year. (In Arizona, mating usually takes place in February and March.) A litter of between one to four young are born after a gestation period of 145 days. The female collared peccary has her litter in a thicket, hollow log, cave or burrow. A few hours after birth, the young can run and in a day or two, they follow their mother when she rejoins the group.

Another species of peccary, the chacoan peccary (*Catagonus wagneri*) was recently "discovered" in the Gran Chaco region of southeastern Bolivia, Paraguay and northern Argentina. The chacoan peccary has long been hunted for food by the native Indians. There is concern that overhunting could cause it to disappear by the end of the century. Protection efforts for the chacoan peccary and the white-lipped peccary are underway by the Convention on International Trade in Endangered Species (CITES). Conservation efforts for the collared peccary have not yet begun.

Range: Arizona and Texas south to northern Argentina.

GOLDEN LION TAMARIN

KEEL-BILLED TOUCAN

COLLARED PECCARY

See illustration on page 87

GOLDEN LION TAMARIN
Leontopithecus rosalia

CURRENTLY, THERE ARE AN ESTIMATED 100-200 GOLDEN LION TAMARINS, 200 GOLDEN-HEADED LION TAMARINS AND 40-100 BLACK LION TAMARINS LEFT IN THE WILD.

Golden lion tamarins live in dense, once abundant rain forests that cover most of the Brazilian state of Rio de Janeiro. The remaining forests are quickly being lumbered to clear them for agriculture and other development. In 1971, efforts were made to establish two tamarin preserves, but the sites were deforested after conservationists failed to secure funding for their purchase. With the continued destruction and fragmentation of their habitat, only 100 to 200 golden lion tamarins still exist in the wild. A planned large-scale agricultural project may eliminate their remaining habitat, thereby threatening extinction of this species.

Members of the marmoset family, golden lion tamarins have long, silky fur the color of gold. The "lion" refers to the lion-like mane of thicker fur on their shoulders and neck. The tamarins grow to a length of from eight to thirteen inches (20-33 cm) with a tail twelve to sixteen inches (30-40 cm) long. The average adult weight is just over a pound and a half (700 grams).

Golden lion tamarins are very agile tree dwellers. They prefer living between ten to thirty-three feet (3-10 meters) off the ground in trees where interlacing branches and vines provide shelter and an abundance of food. They eat a variety of fruits, insects, snails, small lizards and small birds. At night, they sleep in holes in trees or on vines.

Golden lion tamarins live in family groups of three to four individuals. The adult male and female in each group mate for life and are equally dominant. Births occur from September to March (Brazil's warmest and wettest period of the year). After a gestation period of 128 days, a single young is born. The father carries the young tamarin a few days after it is born and is the primary carrier after the third week. Both the male and female take care of the young. Sometimes a juvenile member of the family will also help care for the newborn. Sexual maturity is reached by males at 24 months and by females at 18 months.

Golden lion tamarins are among the world's critically endangered mammals. They are classified as endangered by the United States Department of the Interior (USDI) and the International Union for Conservation of Nature (IUCN). Trade is prohibited by the Convention on International Trade in Endangered Species (CITES).

Two other species of lion tamarins, the golden-headed lion tamarin (*Leontopithecus rosalia chrysomelas*) and the black lion tamarin (*Leontopithecus rosalia chrysopygus*) also are near extinction. Programs to captively breed all three species of lion tamarins have been successful; however without a place in the wild to live, these tamarins face an uncertain future. Stopping the destruction of the rain forests is the most immediate goal for conservationists attempting to save the vanishing lion tamarins.

BRAZIL

See illustration on page 91

KINKAJOU
Potos flavus

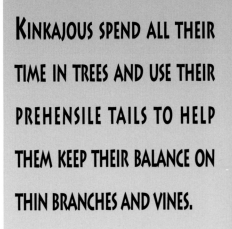

The kinkajou is a member of the extended raccoon family, which also includes raccoons, ringtails and the lesser pandas. Kinkajous are the only member of this family that have a prehensile (grasping) tail. The kinkajou is sometimes called the "honey bear," because it often raids beehives for honey. Kinkajous roam throughout forests from eastern Mexico southward to central Brazil. The main threat to this species is the loss of forest habitat, but kinkajous are also killed by some hunters for their meat and pelts. (The pelt is used for making wallets and belts.)

Kinkajous are brownish with color variations that range into tawny-olive and -yellow. Some individuals have a black line that runs along their back. Kinkajous reach sixteen to thirty inches (40.5 cm to 76 cm) in length and a shoulder height of ten inches (25.4 cm). Males are generally larger than females, and both have long, prehensile tails which reach lengths of up to twenty-two inches (56 cm). They can weigh up to ten pounds (4.5 kg).

Kinkajous have long tongues, which are an adaptation for a diet of fruit and honey. They may also eat insects, small vertebrates, buds and blossoms. While feeding at night, kinkajous give a shrill, quavering scream that can be heard from nearly a mile away.

The kinkajou is a solitary animal, although it is sometimes seen feeding in groups in the same tree. Territories are not defended, but they will emit a "bark" when disturbed. They spend the day in a hollow tree or sometimes lie on a limb or in a tangle of vines. They sleep in the same tree each night.

Female kinkajous come into heat every three months, during which time they can conceive for only two days. During mating the male massages the flanks of the female and licks her chin and her throat glands. After a gestation period of up to 120 days, a single helpless young is born. By four months the baby kinkajou is nearly independent. Males reach full sexual maturity at one and a half years and females are mature at two and a half years. Kinkajous can live to be over twenty years old in captivity.

The future of the kinkajou depends on the future of its habitat. Without the forests of Central and South America, the kinkajou will be just another species added to the endangered list.

KINKAJOUS SPEND ALL THEIR TIME IN TREES AND USE THEIR PREHENSILE TAILS TO HELP THEM KEEP THEIR BALANCE ON THIN BRANCHES AND VINES.

Range: East central Mexico to south central Brazil.

THE SOUTH AMERICAN BOAT-BILLED HERON DIFFERS FROM ALL OTHER HERONS BY ITS WIDE BEAK AND SHORT NECK. THEIR BILLS APPEAR LARGE AND SWOLLEN AND ARE TIPPED WITH A SMALL HOOK.

When the sun goes down, some of the world's most interesting creatures begin to stir. The nocturnal boat-billed heron is certainly one of them. Living from Mexico to northern Argentina, boat-billed herons are threatened by destruction of their wetland habitat and woodland nesting sites.

Pale in color and stocky in build, the heron's most unusual feature is its bill. Because of its peculiar wide and flat beak, it was formerly not grouped with the herons. However, since the beak has basically the same structure as that of other night herons' beaks, it is now considered a true heron. Boat-billed herons also differ from other herons because of their short necks. The total height of a boat-billed heron is eighteen to twenty inches (46-51 cm).

Despite their large eyes, typical of nocturnal animals, boat-billed herons capture their prey by touch rather than sight. They stand crouched and wait for prey, or walk slowly through the shallows to flush their food, mainly shrimp and small fish.

Boat-billed herons nest in trees, bushes or occasionally in reedbeds. They erect a long, feather crest during courtship display, while both males and females clatter their beaks vigorously. The female crouches and stretches out her neck, while the male walks around her. After mating, up to five eggs are laid and incubated for a period of twenty-six days. The nestlings are fed fish, small birds and mammals until they are mature (six to eight weeks).

Boat-billed herons need unpolluted streams and marshes in which to thrive. They also need wetland and woodland habitats for refuge and breeding. Whenever these environments are threatened, the existence of the boat-billed heron is in jeopardy.

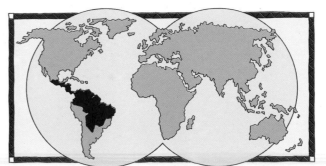

Range: Mexico, Central America south to northern Argentina.

KINKAJOU   BOAT-BILLED HERON   CAVE BAT

CLOUDED LEOPARD
Neofelis nebulosa

THE CLOUDED LEOPARD HAS PROPORTIONATELY THE LONGEST UPPER CANINE TEETH OF ALL THE LIVING CATS.

While the drive to possess the clouded leopard's exquisite fur has generated intense hunting pressure, it is the loss of its forest habitat due to agricultural growth that has critically threatened this species.

Clouded leopards are named for the dark ringed patterns on their fur. Circles, ovals and rosettes resemble cloud shapes floating on a soft fur of white.

Considered unique in the cat family, clouded leopards provide a bridge between the big cats (lions, tigers and cheetahs) and the small cats (ocelots and bobcats). With the big cats they share habits such as their posture when at rest (lying with their forelegs outstretched and their tail straight behind). With the small cats they share features such as a vocal cord structure. Clouded leopards are heavily built, weighing as much as 50 pounds (23 kg), and have short legs and long tails.

Clouded leopards are so agile that they are able to hang on a tree limb with one back paw while dangling down to drop onto their meal. Deer, goats, cattle, pigs, monkeys, birds and young water buffalo are favorite prey for these cats. They are one of the few animals that eat porcupines.

Since clouded leopards are elusive, information about breeding habits has only been observed in captivity. Births in captive populations in Europe and Texas have occurred from March to August. Mothers carry their young for 86-93 days before having anywhere from one to five helpless babies. The young nurse for up to five months.

The clouded leopard is classified as endangered by the United States Department of the Interior (USDI). It is listed as vulnerable by the International Union for Conservation of Nature (IUCN), and trade is prohibited under the Convention on International Trade in Endangered Species (CITES) regulations. However, more work in the areas of conservation and research needs to be done if clouded leopards are to escape the dangers that threaten their survival.

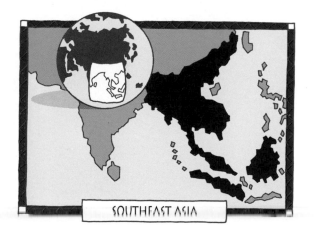

SOUTHEAST ASIA

POISON DART FROG
Dendrobates histrionicus and *Phyllobates terribilis*

POISON DART FROGS HAVE THE MOST COMPLEX SOCIAL BEHAVIOR OF ALL AMPHIBIANS. ADULTS WILL GUARD AND TRANSPORT THE TADPOLES AND DEFEND THEIR TERRITORIES WITH AGGRESSIVE BEHAVIOR, INCLUDING RITUALISTIC COMBAT.

Poison dart frogs (also referred to as poison arrow frogs) live in the tropics of Central and South America. Over the centuries they have been captured by the native peoples who use the toxins in the frogs' skin to poison the tips of their darts. These poison darts are then used for hunting game, such as jaguars, deer, monkeys and birds. It is thought that in the past these small darts poisoned with frog toxin were shot from blowguns in wars with neighboring tribes. While poison dart frogs have been taken for collections and for research, it is the destruction of their rainforest habitat that threatens the survival of these brilliantly colored amphibians.

Poison dart frogs are small, rarely reaching more than two inches (5 cm) in length. Their toe tips have specialized pads for gripping leaves and wet moss. They are extremely bright in color, a common natural warning of toxicity. The skin of the poison dart frog contains some of the most lethal biological toxins known. A mere 0.0000004 oz (0.00001 gram) is enough to kill an average-sized person.

These amphibians live on or close to the forest floor. They eat mainly ants, termites and other small insects or spiders. They defend their territory by being able to intensify their body colors as a warning sign and by giving special territorial calls, usually from rock or tree stump. They are aggressive toward others of their species, often shoving, jumping, biting and fighting one another.

Each *dendrobates* species exhibits its own specialized breeding behavior but typical courtship among poison dart frogs is noisy and active. After initiating courtship with vocalization, a prolonged "trilling sound," the male stimulates its partner by touching, shoving, tapping and mounting. Once the female is aroused, the pair searches for a suitable spawning site. Generally, fertilization occurs outside the female who deposits a few eggs on the ground near water. The male guards the eggs and keeps them wet until they hatch. After two to four weeks, the young tadpoles are carried on the parent's back to water, where the female may feed them with unfertilized eggs.

Some species of poison dart frog are protected by the Convention on International Trade in Endangered Species (CITES II), which controls the exportation of the frogs from their countries of origin. However, many people still try to smuggle these brilliantly colored frogs into the country and raise them in captivity. Poison dart frog population numbers will decline if destruction of the rainforest and smuggling are not curtailed.

Range: Tropical Central and South America

POISON DART FROG WITH RED-EYED TREE FROG

COSTA RICAN CORAL SNAKE

Micrurus nigrocinctus

CORAL SNAKES OCCUPY A VARIETY OF HABITATS AT LOW AND MODERATE ELEVATIONS, FROM DESERTS IN THE SOUTHWEST UNITED STATES AND NORTHERN MEXICO, TO WET AND DRY FORESTS IN THE TROPICS.

The brilliantly colored coral snake of Costa Rica thrives in both the wet and dry tropical forests. Along with other rare and endangered species, the coral snake is threatened by loss of its native habitat. As trees are cleared for development and farmland, a whole ecological system is destroyed.

Coral snakes are easily recognized by the colored ring pattern of their skin. This bright color also signals that the snake is poisonous. A pair of hollow fangs at the front of the upper jawbone conduct venom into the wound. There are also numerous solid teeth in the upper and lower jaw which hold prey while the venom has a chance to work.

The diet of coral snakes includes lizards, frogs, insects, small mammals and other snakes. They forage by slowly crawling and poking through debris on the forest floor. When they recognize their prey, they seize it with a quick forward movement and hold it until it is immobilized by their venom.

Coral snakes exhibit a spectacular defense strategy when disturbed. The tail is coiled, elevated and waved about, while the rest of the body is flattened and erratically snaps back and forth. The head, with the mouth open, is swung from side to side.

Although these snakes are dangerous to humans, they do not bite without being threatened. If left alone in its natural habitat, the coral snake is an important part of a balanced tropical forest ecosystem.

CENTRAL AMERICA

BECAUSE MALE *M. CYPRIS* COMMONLY CHASE AND ASSOCIATE WITH EACH OTHER IT IS BELIEVED THAT THEIR BRIGHT COLORING HAS EVOLVED FOR MALE TO MALE INTERACTION. THEREFORE COLLECTORS WAVE A BRIGHT BLUE SCARF TO DRAW MALES INTO THE RANGE OF THEIR NETS.

The rainforests of Central America are home to some of the most spectacular butterflies in the world. One of these species is *Morpho cypris*. This butterfly depends on the rainforests for its survival. As tropical forests are cleared for human advancement, *M. cypris* disappears.

The male butterfly of this species is an intense chrome blue with a whitish band, females are less spectacularly colored. The male reaches two and a half inches (62 mm) in length, the female three inches (76 mm) in length.

The males of the species fly high above the forest canopy from 10:30 AM to 1 PM, a schedule to which they rigidly adhere; females are not often seen. During their active times, these butterflies feed upon rotting fruits and sap from wounds in trees and vines.

The females lay several eggs on the underside of a leaf. From each egg hatches a hairy, bright red and yellow larva. The larva has several legs, the first set of which contain a special gland that gives off an offensive odor if the larva is disturbed. This protection effectively wards off many bird and amphibian predators. The larva metamorphoses into an adult butterfly within 90 to 120 days after the egg is laid.

The *M. cypris* butterfly is in danger because its habitat is vanishing. Preservation of Central American rainforests is essential to the survival of this spectacular insect species.

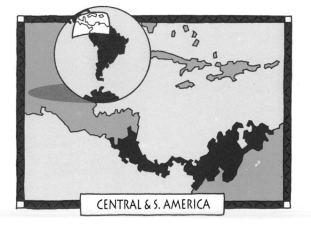

CENTRAL & S. AMERICA

PHILAETHRIA DIDO   MORPHO CYPRUS

BUTTERFLY
Philaethria dido

PHILAETHRIA DIDO ARE DIFFICULT TO CAPTURE, BECAUSE OF THEIR ALERTNESS AND RAPID FLIGHT.

The elaborate wing markings and bright coloration of the butterfly species *Philaethria dido*, create a breathtaking flash of color within the green canopy of the rainforest. This butterfly is found in the wet tropical regions of Mexico south to the Amazon Basin. As rainforests are being destroyed at an increasing rate by humans, this species of butterfly becomes more vulnerable to the process of extinction.

Both male and female *P. dido* are recognized by the green and brown pattern of their upper wings. They are also identified by the typical elongated shape of their forewings. They reach an average length of two inches (51 mm).

The *P. dido* butterfly is seen most often flying high above the rainforest treetops, but they also frequent many species of the tropical passion flower which they use as a food source and as a place to lay their eggs. Occasionally they may be seen on mammal dung deposited on the forest floor.

A female *P. dido* lays eggs on the underside of older leaves of plants growing at ground level. Larvae, which are pale green with blackish-red markings, utilize these leaves in their metamorphosis process.

P. dido is common where rainforests remained undisturbed. However, in places where rainforests have been depleted, this butterfly has vanished.

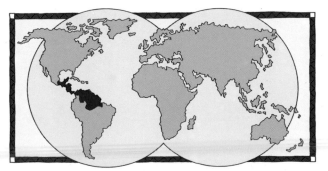

Range: Mexico to the Amazon Basin.

PHILAETHRIA DIDO   MORPHO CYPRUS

AMERICAN FLAMINGO

Phoenicopterus ruber

ONLY TWO GROUPS OF BIRDS, PIGEONS AND FLAMINGOS, FEED THEIR YOUNG ON "MILK." FLAMINGO MILK IS MADE UP OF A RED LIQUID RICH IN FAT AND PROTEIN.

In the past, human predation and exploitation of adults and eggs took a heavy toll on American flamingo populations. Today, habitat destruction and fragmentation by encroaching development are eliminating the flamingos' breeding and feeding grounds. Especially important is the fact that flamingos are colonial birds that need to breed in large congregations of their own kind. Undisturbed areas large enough for breeding colonies are quickly disappearing.

The American flamingo, often called the "greater flamingo," is soft-crimson in color with a long neck and long legs. Flamingos' legs are longer in proportion to their bodies than that of any other bird. Males are larger than females weighing eight pounds (3.6 kg) compared to the female's 6.5 pounds (2.9 kg). Both sexes can reach 50 inches (127 cm) in length and have a 60 inch (152 cm) wingspan. American flamingos have been known to stand as high as six and a half feet (198 cm) tall.

The flamingo's distinctive curved bill serves as a filtering system for feeding. When it bends its neck down, it immerses the bill with the top side down in shallow water. The tongue acts as a piston, pushing rich organic bottom ooze through the bill at a rate of three or four cycles per second. This muddy water passes through a filtering plate inside the bill where algae, bacteria, diatoms and tiny fishes are extracted for food.

American flamingos are social birds and gather in flocks of thousands of pairs. Ritual dis-

play behavior consists of the same movements they use each day for stretching and preening, but more exaggerated and more stiffly performed. "Head flagging," where they stretch their necks into the air, is followed by "wing saluting," when they flap their wings by their sides. American flamingos also include other movements in this ritual. When a few birds begin to display, their behavior encourages the rest of the flock to do the same in a breathtaking flash of colorful motion. Group displays help encourage the colony to mate at the same time in order to ensure a stable breeding season.

American flamingos mate for life (as long as 50 years). The pair bond is strong and both birds help make the nest and raise the young. Their nests are tall mounds of dried mud with a slight indentation at the top to hold a single egg which is incubated by both sexes. After hatching, the chick is fed a nutritious red "milk" produced by both parents. In four to six weeks. the chick is herded from the nest into a large group with other chicks where it stays until it has fully matured eleven weeks later.

The International Union for Conservation of Nature (IUCN) has recognized the American flamingo as a threatened species. As an example of habitat restoration, the salt industry in southern France has created man-made lagoons which are being accepted by the flamingos in that area. Still, more conservation efforts must be encouraged to preserve the many subspecies of flamingos that remain in jeopardy.

YUCATAN & BAHAMAS

I am very fond of this painting because I was working on it until the day before my youngest daughter, Amy, was born. I resumed work on it two weeks later. My studio has always been at home, so I have the luxury of painting any time that I want, and yet still do "mom" things like helping with homework etc. Often my children will do their homework right in my studio. The extra activity has never bothered me, although my favorite time to paint is at night after the children have gone to bed. — L.R.

RAINBOW LIZARDS ARE ALSO KNOWN AS "WHIPTAILS" OR "RACERUNNERS."

The rainbow lizard is adaptable to a wide range of natural habitats. When forests are cleared for lumber, agriculture or for other development, however, small creatures, such as the rainbow lizard, cannot adapt.

Rainbow lizards are brown in color with yellow stripes running down their backs and tails. In the male, vivid, iridescent blue coloring appears on the outer edges of the tail, head, nose and feet. Rainbow lizards reach a body length of twelve inches (30 cm), with a tail at least as long as the body.

The rainbow lizard is a very agile ground-dweller mainly active during the day when it feeds upon insects, grasshoppers, spiders and other small prey that make up its diet.

Mating takes place when a sexually active male attempts to straddle a female. If she is responsive, he rubs his hip region against her back while nipping at her neck. If mating is successful, then early in the summer the female rainbow lizard will lay four to six eggs in a shallow depression or under rocks. The young lizards hatch in eight to ten weeks.

Rainbow lizards are not in immediate threat of extinction and have not been designated as rare or endangered. They are, however, one of the many species threatened because their environment is being destroyed.

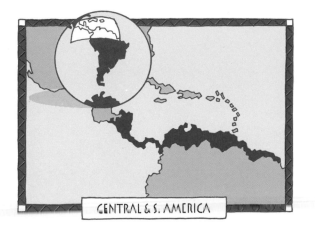

CENTRAL & S. AMERICA

GECKO   RAINBOW LIZARD

GECKO
Family *Gekkonidae*

GECKOS CAN SHED THEIR TAILS IF THREATENED BY A PREDATOR. WHEN THE TAIL IS RELEASED, ONLY A STUMP REMAINS. A NEW TAIL IS GROWN WITHIN A SHORT PERIOD.

Throughout the world, wherever there is a warm climate, at least one species of gecko will be found. From deserts to rainforests to islands, this small "talkative" lizard will broadcast its variety of calls. Geckos are harmless to humans and, in fact, are considered good luck to have around. Since humans are not a direct threat to geckos, these lizards roam freely in developed areas. Gecko populations are, however, susceptible to climatic changes and rainforest destruction.

Many geckos have webbed feet with special "bristles" underneath. Each bristle has a saucer-shaped end plate, or spatula, which grips even the smoothest surfaces. Therefore, most geckos can climb anywhere, even on vertical panes of glass and on ceilings. Their tails are modified under the tip, with hair-like projections similar to those on the toes, so the tail also can help hold the gecko to a surface. In some gecko species, the tail is prehensile and can be used for grasping objects.

Usually active at night, geckos can eat a wide variety of insects and small crustaceans. It is common for geckos to enter houses in the evening where bright lights have attracted insects. Some geckos will also eat small mammals and birds, while others prefer nectar and sweet sap from trees.

The female gecko will lay one or two eggs. The eggs have a tough, white shell and are laid under stones, behind window shutters, or under bark. A baby gecko breaks out of its egg by piercing it with sharply pointed paired egg teeth at the tip of the snout. The egg teeth drop off shortly after hatching. Communal egg laying sites are typical of many species of gecko.

While the gecko family in general is not immediately imperiled, many species of geckos live in threatened environments. Many island gecko species are found nowhere else. On Madagascar, in particular, all of the island's fauna and flora is threatened by overfarming and destruction of forest habitat.

Gecko populations should be monitored since any decline in their populations could indicate trouble for the less adaptable species.

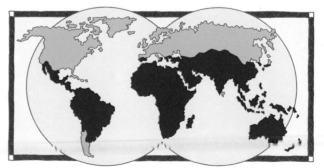

Range: Worldwide, mainly in warm and tropical climates.

GECKO   RAINBOW LIZARD

I wanted the background of this painting to have a striped effect, imitating the coats of the young cubs. Since tigers rely heavily on their stripes for camouflage, the trees represent shelter & security, or perhaps even an abstract image of their protective mother. I did not want the cubs to look fearful. In fact, the little guy on the right seems to be quite content to focus on some small thing hidden in the grass. — L.R.

TIGER
Panthera tigris

TIGERS ARE EXTREMELY GOOD SWIMMERS, EASILY CROSSING RIVERS 5 MILES (8 KM) WIDE. THEY HAVE BEEN KNOWN TO SWIM A DISTANCE OF UP TO 18 MILES (29 KM) BEFORE STOPPING TO REST.

While tigers are dangerous to people, they pose more of a threat to livestock. Consequently, tigers have been trapped, poisoned and hunted in great numbers. In addition, sport hunting for tigers became especially popular after World War II. Finally, during the 1960s the commercial trade in tiger skins intensified. By 1977 a tiger pelt brought as much as $4,250 in the United States.

Tigers are powerful animals. They are fearless, strong and stunning to behold. On an average, a tiger is almost seven feet (210 cm) long and has a 2.5 foot (76 cm) long tail. Males weigh in at 535 pounds (243 kg), while females average 295 pounds (134 kg). The Siberian tiger (*P. tigris altaica*), a subspecies of tiger living in southeastern Siberia, Manchuria and Korea is the largest living cat in the world.

A tiger's diet consists mainly of antelope, pig, deer, buffalo and gaur. Relying especially on their sense of hearing, tigers stalk their prey approaching from the side or rear, then kill the animal by a throat bite (which strangles the prey) or a bite to the back of the neck. Tigers have an incredible roar that is used to announce the kill. After the kill, they can consume up to 88 pounds (40 kg) of meat at one time.

Tigers are essentially solitary animals, but courting pairs and females with young are seen together. Tigers seem to accept others of their species, but avoid one another by maintaining territories. After mating season females have two or three cubs after a gestation period of 105 days. They give birth in caves, rocky crevices or in dense vegetation. The young stay with their mother for about two years and reach maturity in three to five years.

With the expansion of human populations, logging of forests and elimination of natural prey, there is intensifying conflict between people and tigers. While some tiger populations have increased slightly as a result of conservation efforts, only 6000 to 8000 tigers are thought to exist. The tiger is classified as endangered by the United States Department of the Interior (USDI) and by the International Union for Conservation of Nature. Tigers also are protected by the Convention on International Trade in Endangered Species (CITES).

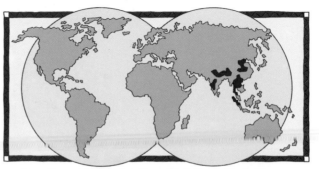

Range: Eastern Asia, India, Indochina and the Indonesian islands of Sumatra.

KOALA
Phacolarctos cinereus

THE KOALA BELONGS TO THE MARSUPIAL FAMILY. MARSUPIALS ARE DISTINGUISHED BY THEIR UNIQUE REPRODUCTIVE SYSTEM IN WHICH THE BABY LIVES IN THE MOTHER'S POUCH DURING MUCH OF ITS DEVELOPMENTAL PHASE.

Until the early 1900s there were millions of koalas in southeastern Australia. In the early years of the century, increased access to their range encouraged hunting. Demand grew quickly for their beautiful, warm, durable fur. In 1924, two million koala skins were exported from southern Australia. In 1927, economic pressure in the state of Queensland prompted an open season on koalas resulting in an additional 600,000 animals being killed.

With soft fur, a big head and round fuzzy ears, the koala's endearing features make it one of the world's most beloved animals. Weighing between 9 and 33 pounds (4-15 kg), they range from 23-33 inches (58-84 cm) in length when mature. Their tail is almost nonexistent, with only an evolutionary remnant of a fuller tail remaining.

Koalas have cheek pouches and a special digestive tract which allow them to eat bulky, fibrous eucalyptus leaves that form the main portion of their diet. They ingest soil and gravel which help break down tough plant material. There are more than 500 different species of eucalyptus trees, and koalas feed upon at least three dozen. They have been known to eat mistletoe and box (Tristania) leaves in the wild.

As a result of their diet, koalas are confined to eucalyptus forests. They are crepuscular (more likely awake at dawn and at dusk) and arboreal (living in trees), coming down only to shuffle slowly to another food tree or to ingest a little soil or gravel for digestive purposes. They are mainly solitary and will savagely attack another animal trespassing in their territory.

During breeding season, males may attempt to defend a territory containing several females. Female koalas will give birth, after a short gestation period of 35 days, to a single baby weighing as little as 0.013 ounce (0.36 grams). Being marsupial mammals, the undeveloped young stay in a pouch located on the mother's stomach for five to seven months, and are weaned at six to twelve months. Full physical maturity for female koalas is four years and males reach maturity after five. The normal life span for a koala is ten years.

Since the 1920s, intensive conservation efforts have allowed for recovery of the koala in some parts of southeastern Australia. The breeding and transplantation of thousands of koalas by the Victoria Fisheries and Wildlife Division has helped in this. However, continued conservation efforts are needed to protect the habitat of this beloved species.

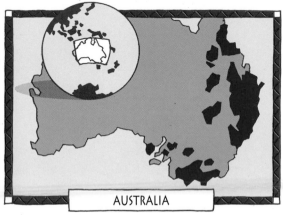

AUSTRALIA

L. Regan '91©

INDEX

*Page numbers in **boldface** refer to illustrations.*

Austin, O.L., Jr., *Birds of the World,* Golden Press, 1961.

Burghardt, G.M. and A.S. Rand, eds., *Iguanas of the World; Their Behavior, Ecology and Conservation,* Noyes Publ., 1982.

Burt, W.H. and R.P. Grossenheider, *A Field Guide to the Mammals,* Peterson Field Guide Series, Houghton Mifflin, 1976.

Burton, J., ed., *The Atlas of Endangered Species,* MacMillan Publ. Co., 1991.

Campbell, J.A. and W.W. Lamar, *The Venomous Reptiles of Latin America,* Cornell Univ. Press, 1989.

Convention of International Trade in Endangered Species of Wild Flora and Fauna, Appendices I, II and III to the CITES, U.S. Dept. of the Interior, USFWS, 1991.

Crump, M.L., "Apparent Decline of the Golden Toad: Underground or Extinct?", *Copeia* (2): 413-420. 1992.

Crump, M.L., "Life History Consequences of Feeding Versus Non-feeding in a Facultative Non-feeding Toad Larva," *Oecologia,* 78:486-489, 1992.

Devries, P.J., *The Butterflies of Costa Rica and Their Natural History: Papilionidae, Pieridae, Nymphalidae,* Princeton Univ, Press, 1987.

Duellman, W.E., *Biology of Amphibians,* McGraw-Hill, 1985.

Embery, J. and E. Lucaire, *Joan Embery's Collection of Amazing Animal Facts,* Delacorte Press, 1983.

Forshaw, J.M., *Parrots of the World,* T.F.H. Publications, 1977.

Grzimek, B., *Animal Life Encyclopedia,* Van Nostrand Reinhold, 1972.

Grzimek, B., *Grzimek's Encyclopedia of Mammals,* McGraw-Hill, 1990.

Hall, E.R., and K.R. Kelson, *The Mammals of North America,* The Ronald Press Co., 1959.

Halliday, T.R. and K. Adler, *Reptiles and Amphibians (All the World's Animals),* Torstar Books [Equinox (Oxford) Ltd.], 1986.

Haltenorth, T. and H. Diller, *A Field Guide to the Mammals of Africa Including Madagascar,* Collins, 1986.

Handasayde, Lee A.K.K.A. and G.E. Sanson, eds., *The Biology of the Koala,* 1991.

Janzen, D.H., ed., *Costa Rican Natural History,* Univ. of Chicago Press, 1983.

Johnsgard, P.A., *Cranes of the World,* Indiana Univ. Press, 1983.

Knox, M.L., "No Nation an Island," *Sierra,* 74(3):78-84, 1989.

Laurenson, M.K., T. Caro, and M. Borner, "Female Cheetah Reproduction," *National Geographic Research and Exploration,* vol. 8(1):64-75, 1992.

Lee, K.A., K.A. Handasyde, and G.D. Sanson, eds., *The Biology of the Koala,* Surrey Beatty, 1991.

Low, R., *Endangered Parrots,* Sterling Publ. Co., 1984.

Lowe, D.W., et al, eds., *The Official World Wildlife Fund Guide to Endangered Species of North America,* Beacham Publ., 1990.

Macdonald, D., ed., *The Encyclopedia of Mammals,* Facts on File, Inc. [Equinox (Oxford) Ltd.], 1984.

Mattison, C., *Lizards of the World,* Facts on File, Inc., 1989.

Morcombe, M., *Australian Marsupials and Other Native Mammals,* Summit Books, 1980.

Myers, C.W. and J.W. Daly, "Dart-poison Frogs," *Scientific American,* 248(2):120-133, 1983.

Nowak, R.M., *Walker's Mammals of the World,* 5th Edition, John Hopkins Univ. Press, 1991.

Obst, F.J., et al, J.G. Walls, ed., English Language Edition, *The Completely Illustrated Atlas of Reptiles and Amphibians for the Terrarium,* T.F.H. Publ., 1988.

Perrins, C.M., *The Illustrated Encyclopedia of Birds, The Definitive Reference to Birds of the World,* Prentice Hall Press, 1990.

Perrins, C.W., and A. Middleton, *The Encyclopedia of Birds,* Facts on File, Inc. [Equinox (Oxford) Ltd.], 1985.

Ryder, Oliver A., "The Giant Panda is a Bear," *Zoonooz,* 60(8):16-17, 1987.

Skutch, A.F., *Birds of Tropical America,* Univ. of Texas Press, 1983.

Sprackland, R.G., *Giant Lizards,* T.F.H. Publications, 1992.

Terres, J.K., *The Audubon Society Encyclopedia of North American Birds,* Knopf, 1980.

Thornback, J., and M. Jenkins, compilers, *The IUCN Mammal Red Data Book; Part I; Threatened Mammalian Taxa of the Americas and the Australasian Zoogeographic Region (Excluding Cetaceans),* IUCN, Gland Switzerland, 1982.

Troyer, K., Diet Selection and Digestion in Iguana Iguana: The Importance of Age and Nutrient Requirements, *Oecologia,* 61:201-207, 1984.

U.S. Dept. of the Interior, USFWS, *Endangered and Threatened Wildlife and Plants,* 50 CFR 17.11 & 17.12, July 15, 1991.

Whitney, S., *Western Forests,* The Audubon Society Nature Guides, Knopf, 1985.

Williams, J.G. and N. Arlott, *A Field Guide to the Birds of East and Central Africa,* Colins, 1985.